Embrace *His* Call

Embrace *His* Call

Be More Than A Believer

Joy Hughes Gruits

First printing: 2019
Printed in the United States of America

ISBN: 9781092591812

Publisher contact: embracehiscall.com; joy.gruits@gmail.com

To Patricia Beall Gruits

who was more than a mother-in-law to me.
She was a spiritual mentor,
modeling what it means to be more than a believer:
to be a disciple of Christ—
a devoted follower of Jesus.

Table of Contents

Part I: Knowing Him

Part II: Tough Love

Part III: Transforming Power

INTRODUCTION

There was a polite and quiet uneasiness in the car. Gazing out the window I wondered how I had gotten myself into this situation. As our team neared our destination, my heart beat faster and my stomach filled with butterflies. Security fences and stark rectangular buildings came into view. Straight ahead was the maximum-security prison with its gray admissions building. After signing in and an inter-minable wait, it was our turn to enter the sally port, the secure chamber which serves as the entry point into the prison. The automatic sliding glass doors opened and two security officers were ready to proceed with the pat-down procedure. Once completed, we were given personal protection devices—PPDs. If we felt threatened, we were to pull the string and the officers would come running. Now my heart was really pounding. *If we were given PPDs, then surely there must be a genuine need for them.* I carefully clipped mine to the waist of my slacks, ensuring the little string was easily accessible.

An officer then led us to an outdoor courtyard where a few bare bleachers had been erected. As the inmates filled the stands on this hot August Saturday, the guest evangelist began to share her life's story—a testimony of God's grace and deliverance. Following her message, our team was to meet and pray with the inmates.

As I scanned the bleachers, I couldn't help but look at the faces of men who had lived lives so foreign to mine. The evangelist wrapped up her message, and my anxiety grew because I knew I soon would be asked to interact and pray for these men, some who towered over me. My hand quickly double-checked the PPD—*where was that string?* But as the inmates came forward for prayer, as I talked and prayed with them, all thoughts of the PPD disappeared. I was filled with a genuine compassion for them as they shared their hunger for the Lord. Yet of all the inmates I spoke to and prayed with that day, one stood out most distinctly. I asked him what he wanted me to pray for, and his heartfelt response was this: "I am believer. I know I am saved. But how do I live what I believe?" His struggle was not about believing or having faith. His struggle was about living his faith. He didn't know how to be a disciple—a devoted follower of Christ.

Twelve Followers

In the first century there were twelve well-known followers of Christ. The three best-known among them were Peter, James, and John; good Jewish boys who had been properly schooled in the local synagogue. Most likely they had studied and memorized the Scriptures, the basis of their education, until they entered the family business—fishing. Although no longer being educated in the synagogue, these three young men still possessed a spiritual hunger. They attended the desert camp meetings where John the Baptist preached about a special rabbi, the Messiah, who would establish a new kingdom on earth. They were intrigued, but there was no chance they could ever be one of his chosen disciples. They weren't scholars. They hadn't advanced to the next level of rabbinical training. They were mere fishermen. But one incredible day, this special rabbi approached them at their nets. "Come, follow me," he said. His invitation: Be my disciples.

To be chosen by a rabbi was considered a high calling, similar to a student today being accepted into a prestigious university. So to be chosen by *this* rabbi, even one who hadn't come up through the traditional rabbinical ranks, was an honor. After all, this rabbi was special—unique in wisdom, insight, and power. Their response was immediate. They left behind their livelihood and embraced the call to follow Jesus, to be his disciples.

For more than three years, these three men along with nine more, saw Jesus perform miracles of healing, deliverance, and resurrection. They heard him teach the multitudes and then received private interpretations of his messages. They watched in awe as Jesus confounded the Pharisees, the Sadducees, and teachers of the law with his wisdom and knowledge. And as they *followed*, they received the full revelation of who Jesus was. As they *followed*, their faith matured; their lives were changed.

More Than A Believer

Perhaps the best-known verse in the Bible is John 3:16. The profound words of this verse define the very essence of our Christian faith.

> For God so loved the world that he gave his one and only Son, that whoever believes in him shall not perish but have eternal life.

Simply stated, if we believe in Jesus Christ as our Savior, we are saved from a destiny of eternal damnation and separation from God, and in exchange we receive the gift of eternal life with him in heaven. This gift of salvation is ours as a genuine expression of God's love for us. The initial work of salvation, however, is not meant to be an endpoint, but rather the beginning point of *following* Christ. It is to be the beginning of our spiritual journey, not the destination. The believing is where the *following* is to commence.

This is where that inmate struggled. It wasn't the *believing*, it was the *following*. He didn't realize he had to choose to embrace Christ's call to *be* a disciple, to be a devoted follower of Jesus. Because he wasn't *following*, he wasn't being changed from the inside out. His faith wasn't maturing. And this choice to *follow* Jesus, to be his disciple, is a choice each one of us must make.

So how do we make that choice? How do we embrace his call and follow Jesus? We can't follow him through the streets of Judea, Galilee, or Samaria. We can't follow him into the local synagogues to hear him preach. We can't follow him to the outskirts of town where he performs miracles of healing and deliverance. We can't sit at his feet on the mountainside while he explains the meaning of the parables. But there is a way we can follow Jesus today. We can follow him through the Scriptures. We can hear his voice through his Word—which brings us to the purpose of this book.

In the following pages, it is my prayer that you will hear the Lord's voice in the stories and lessons that I share from the Bible, that they will move you beyond the step of believing in Jesus and toward the action of following him. Just as Jesus invited the Twelve to follow him, so he calls us—he calls you—with that same invitation: to be *followers* of Christ. Each chapter lesson will help bridge the gap between what we believe and how we live as his disciples. The initial lessons focus on the power of God's love and our identity as his child, as well as his expectations and how he reveals his plan for our lives. The "Tough Love" section addresses adversity and the importance of repentance. The final section of the book, "Transforming Power," deals with vital spiritual truths that foster spiritual maturity.

If you are a new believer, I applaud you for your desire to embrace his call to be a disciple of Jesus. May these lessons birth in you a deep devotion to him. If you are a believer who has already made the choice to follow Jesus, these lessons may not be new to you, but it is my hope that they will inspire you afresh, strengthen your faith, and draw you closer to Jesus.

May they kindle in us all a deeper commitment to Christ—to fully embrace *his call!*

Author's Note:

1) At the end of each chapter is a lesson summary with a "Chapter Challenge" designed to help you apply each lesson.

2) All scripture quotations are taken the New International Version (NIV) of the Bible unless otherwise noted. For a scripture quotation within a paragraph, the scripture reference will be provided as a footnote. Italics and parentheses within a quoted scripture are mine to provide emphasis or clarity.

3) The New International Version (NIV) and the New Living Translation (NLT) of the Bible do not capitalize pronouns referring to God, Jesus, or the Holy Spirit. Because these versions are most frequently cited in this book, I adopted the same convention, not in any way to diminish the deity of God, but rather for consistency of usage.

Part I

Knowing Him

Chapter 1

Embrace His Love

"Jesus *loves me* this I know, for the Bible tells me so!" These lyrics have been sung by thousands of children for generations, and I was one of those children. In a small, wood-framed church in a little-known town outside of Detroit, I learned every verse of this song along with the hand motions. But when I was seven, those words became more than a song; they became truth for me. One Sunday morning, without my pastor extending an invitation to come forward for prayer, I was compelled to kneel at the altar of this little church, insisting that my pastor pray for me as I accepted Jesus Christ as my Savior. On that day, the message of that simple song, "*Jesus Loves Me*," became a reality in my life. The God who so loved the *world* that he gave his only Son to die for it saw the "me" in that world. That truth planted in my heart a desire to follow Jesus—this One who "loves me so!"

Regrettably, often truths that we so easily embrace as children we struggle with as adults. We reason that it makes sense for God to know and love important believers—the pastors of megachurches or well-known evangelists—but me? Surely there are more important people than me in whom he is interested, for whom he loves and cares. Yet all we have to do is look at one small moment on the cross when Jesus sees his mother to catch a glimpse of the Lord's infinite love and compassion expressed in an incredibly personal way. In this brief moment on the cross, Jesus reveals the depth of his individual love, confirming that his invitation to *follow* him is not just for a chosen few or the spiritual elite; it is for each one of us. Because he loves us. He loves me. He loves you.

A Sorrowful Day

It was a sorrowful day as Mary stood looking at her son, her heart breaking. He had been beaten so badly that his swollen, blood-stained face no longer resembled her Jesus. She winced as she caught a glimpse of his back: nothing but bloody, shredded strands of flesh. His breathing was labored. His bones were out of joint. She cringed as people around her mocked and jeered at him, disparaging his identity, denouncing his calling. She mourned as she watched Roman soldiers gambling over who would get his discarded clothes.

Yet there she stood, looking at her son, seeing with a mother's eyes the suffering he was enduring. How difficult it must have been for her to stand near that cross, keeping vigil for hours, watching him suffer and then die. To endure what she was witnessing, Mary must have reached down into her heart for those memories that she had pondered so many times. Memories that filled her heart with joy.

How many times as Jesus was growing up had she revisited the moment when the Angel Gabriel appeared to her. How overwhelmed she had been—and still was—that God the Father had chosen her to birth the Savior of the world. What awe filled her heart! And when she had been the brunt of gossip, she would comfort herself with the joy of that memory. When Jesus was ridiculed, she would rebuff the sting by remembering the shepherds who came to worship infant Jesus. When he was rejected, she revisited the majestic visit of the regal wise men bearing precious gifts to honor her son. How amazed Mary had been when Jesus, as a boy, confounded and astonished the rabbis by his depth of knowledge and understanding of the Scriptures. How many times had a smile come across her face whenever she recalled his first miracle—the one she had prompted him to perform—the turning of water into wine. How proud she had been to see the crowds following him. What joy she felt as she witnessed suffering people receive miracles of healing and deliverance. But always in the back of her mind were the prophetic words spoken by Simeon the prophet on the day she and Joseph brought infant Jesus to the temple. Yes, Mary had marveled when Simeon confirmed that Jesus was the promised Savior. Yet how she trembled in her heart when he turned to her and said, "A sword shall pierce your soul, for this child shall be rejected by many . . ."[1]

Now that moment had arrived. As Mary stood near the cross, she knew that prophecy was being fulfilled. Her heart, once filled with overflowing joy, was now pierced with the sword of sorrow—the sorrow of a mother witnessing her child suffer.

A Small Moment

But in the midst of her son's suffering there is this small moment that speaks volumes about our Lord. It is often overlooked because of the magnitude of what Jesus was accomplishing on the cross. It is a small moment tucked into the Scriptures which documents the last few minutes of Jesus' life.

> Near the cross of Jesus stood his mother . . . When Jesus saw his mother there, and the disciple whom he loved standing nearby, he said to her, "Woman, here is your son!" Then he said to the disciple, "Here is your mother!"
> (John 19:25-30)

On the cross, God the Father was pouring into Jesus the sins of all humanity—past, present, and future. He who had never committed a sin was becoming all sin. He who had never experienced guilt, shame, or condemnation was now experiencing it all—the emotional and spiritual pain of sin. Because of the cross, Jesus would make possible eternal salvation and divine fellowship with God for all mankind. But while he was accomplishing this tremendous work of redemption, there was a small yet significant moment when Jesus saw his mother.

---

[1] Luke 2:24 TLB

Although his body was racked with pain, as his gaze rested upon her face, he saw her pain. Her sorrow. Her grief. Even in the throes of his own suffering, he was moved by *her* suffering. Even though Jesus was the Son of God dying for all humanity, he was still mindful that he was Mary's eldest son, the one according to Jewish tradition who was responsible for her care.

So, what did Jesus do? In essence he said, "John, take care of my mother! Take care of her as if she were your very own mother." He bestowed upon John the responsibility of the eldest son. And standing near the cross, Mary heard these words, confirming to her his love and care.

All Things

Following this intimate moment of compassion, we read,

> After this, Jesus, knowing that *all things* were now accomplished . . . he said, It is finished: and he bowed his and his head and gave up his ghost (spirit).
> (John 19:28-30 KJV)

Jesus couldn't die until *all* things were accomplished. And ensuring his mother was taken care of was part of the *all things*. While completing the great work of salvation, Jesus did not dismiss his spirit, did not declare "it is finished," until he had completed this small, intimate act of love and compassion. What comfort those words must have brought to Mary, not because John would now provide for her, but because this act was an expression of Jesus' *singular* and *significant* love for her.

What comfort and joy we, too, can draw from this small moment! We live in a world where we are bombarded with global news that overwhelms us—unwinnable wars, fragile economies, environmental disasters, escalating violence. Major problems are on every side. Yet from this personal moment we witness at the cross, we gain the assurance that the Lord's concern and compassion extends even to our personal moments of sorrow and need —because the love Jesus had for his mother is the same love he has for us, that he has for you!

> And I am convinced that nothing can ever separate us from God's love. Neither death nor life, neither angels or demons, neither our fears for today nor our worries about tomorrow . . . No power in the sky above or in the earth below, indeed, in all creation will ever be able to separate us from the love of God that is revealed in Christ Jesus our Lord.
> (Romans 8:38-39 NLT)

His love is that great. His love is that profound. A love he has for each one of us.

A Diagnosis

My older sister was relatively young when she was diagnosed with Alzheimer's. It wasn't significant news on the world stage. After all, thousands are diagnosed every day with this debilitating disease. No, her dire prognosis didn't rock this world, but it rocked our little world. Her future was now filled with uncertainty. But one thing was certain: she knew God still loved her.

This disease was not a sign that God's hand of favor and blessing had been withdrawn from her life. She knew disease and death are part of the human experience in our broken world. Certainly, during those very first days after she had heard that devastating word, "*Alzheimer's*," her inclination was to withdraw into a cocoon of self-pity and hopelessness. But instead she made a choice—a pivotal choice. She chose to turn to the One she knew who loved her. And he spoke to her heart reassuring words that brought comfort and strength: "I will be with you through the journey. You will never be alone."

My sister's health issue may be insignificant in comparison to the issues of this world or even to the heartache and pain others are suffering, but I know with full assurance that she is not insignificant to Jesus. But some may ask, "If God loves her, why doesn't he heal her?" God reveals his love for us not just by removing problems and hardships that are part of life, but by strengthening and comforting us as we face adversity. My sister's testimony is that he is with her in this journey. He has not abandoned her; he continues to comfort her with his loving peace. She is significant to Jesus. She is precious to him. She is loved.

Lesson One

To the world, at the work place, even within our own families, we may feel insignificant and unloved, but we are never insignificant to the Lord. We are loved. While Jesus was becoming the answer to the needs of all mankind, he cared about Mary's need. This very personal act exemplifies the Lord's desire to extend his immeasurable love to us in very personal and individual ways. And, his desire is that we will *embrace* this profound love and choose to *follow* him.

Chapter Challenge

- Take a moment right now to pray audibly or to write a prayer thanking Jesus for loving you and dying on the cross for you.

- Express in your prayer how grateful you are that by caring for Mary as he was dying, he provided an example of the depth of his love—a love that makes *you* significant to him, that makes *you* precious to him.

- Recall a moment where you felt seen by the Lord.

- Ask the Lord to reveal his love for you in some perceptible way today.

- If you have never done so, declare your desire to follow him—to be his disciple.

Chapter 2

Embrace Your Identity

Childhood memories create indelible imprints on our lives. Some remind us of a painful moment or a broken heart; others take us back to a humorous incident or proud event. Yet the most precious memories are those that reassure us we are loved.

My younger sister and I attended elementary school together. When I was in sixth grade, she was in third. In her class was a boy named Barry, who had a crush on her. So, what does a third-grade boy do when he likes a girl? He pesters her to no end. And that is exactly what Barry did. Whether it was lunchtime, class time, or recess, he chased and bothered my sister at every turn. One day as we were walking home from school, Barry changed his game plan. Instead of pestering my sister, he turned his attention to me. Unexpectedly, Barry jumped in front of me and latched on with an unrelenting bear hug. Using all my strength, I tried to get him to release his grip, but to no avail. As I struggled, suddenly I felt his weight being lifted up and away from me. Then I heard a booming, authoritative yet familiar voice declare, "From now on, leave my daughters alone."

It was my father.

Without our knowledge, he was following us in his truck, and when he saw Barry jump on me, he jumped into action! Whenever I recall that moment of rescue, I'm moved by the depth of love my father had for us. Why did he love us so much? Because we were his children. Yet, my father's love is but a small reflection of the love our heavenly Father has for us. For we are more than an acquaintance or even a friend of God; we are *his children*. The Scriptures state: "His (God's) unchanging plan has always been to adopt us into his own family . . ."[1] Adoption was in the heart of God the Father: it was part of his salvation plan. Not just to save us, but to adopt us as his children. Jesus Christ is the firstborn, the only begotten Son, but we are his adopted children. Incredible! Especially if you consider the power of adoption.

Several years ago, my daughter and son-in-law entered a courtroom with an eight-month-old baby in their arms. After almost two years of waiting, they had joyfully accepted Scarlet into their lives when she was just three days old. For the next eight months, however, they were regarded by law only as Scarlet's guardians. During that time, they completed endless paperwork, were evaluated with home visits, and waited with anxiety as each hurdle was completed. Finally, a court date was set for Scarlet's official adoption.

As they sat before the judge with Scarlet in their arms, the judge asked if they were willing to accept total parental responsibility for her—to care for her physical, intellectual, emotional, and spiritual well-being. "Yes!" was their emphatic response! Then the judge pronounced with a succinct but powerful statement that Scarlet was *their* daughter. What they had believed in their hearts was now official. They were her parents without exclusions or disclaimers, and she now possessed *all* the rights and benefits of a begotten child.

Children of God

The apostle John wrote: "But to all who believed him (Jesus) and accepted him, he gave the right to become the children of God."[2] If you believe in Jesus Christ and have accepted him as your Savior, then with all certainty you have been adopted as a child of God. Not

---

[1] Eph. 1:5 TLB
[2] John 1:12 NLT

a foster child, not a step-child, but *his* child. In fact, Paul builds upon this truth by stating that "since we are his children, we are his heirs. In fact, together with Christ we are heirs of God's glory."[3] No exclusions, no disclaimers. We belong to him and will share in Christ's spiritual blessings and inheritance.

It is imperative that you never forget your identity—who you are, to whom you belong, and by whom you are loved. And always remember that as your loving Father, he has made provision for your eternal future, for your eternal inheritance. But there is more. He has also made provision for what you need in your life today, because he has prepared daily bread for his children.

Daily Bread

When the disciples asked Jesus to teach them how to pray, he responded by giving them a pattern for prayer known as the Lord's Prayer. And tucked between the instructions to pray according to God's will and to forgive so that we can be forgiven, Jesus referred to this provision of "daily bread." The exact prayer words are these: "Give us today our daily bread."[4] These words encourage us to ask God daily for the provision we need—whether our needs are physical, emotional, or spiritual. We have permission to lay our requests before him without hesitation. Yet there is an incident in the Bible that adds a layer of meaning to our prayer for "daily bread."

A Canaanite woman approached Jesus, crying for help, asking him to heal her daughter. This was a bold request because the woman was a "non-Jew." She was a Gentile, one whose heritage did not descend from Abraham the Jewish patriarch. Therefore, at this point in history, she was not regarded as one of God's chosen people. And since Jesus' ministry at this time was as a Jew to the Jewish people, it is not surprising that Jesus did not respond to her request. Yet she persisted. Even as the disciples tried to turn her away, she kept crying

---

[3] Rom. 8:17
[4] Matthew 6:11

out to Jesus. Finally he turned to her and said, "I was sent only to help God's lost sheep—the people of Israel."[5]

Jesus gave her the reason that he couldn't respond to her need. This season for miracles of healing and deliverance was for the Jews, not the Gentiles. Yet this woman was undeterred. She cried, "Lord, help me!" Jesus was moved by her response, but persisted in his answer: "It's not right to take the children's bread and cast it to dogs." Her response is startling to us, but not to her. "Yes, Lord, yet even the little dogs eat of the crumbs which fall from their master's table."[6] This woman understood the culture of her time. She acknowledged her place in this society. She knew she had no right to receive the miracle of healing that belonged to the Jews. But she had such faith in Jesus's power that she believed she needed only a "crumb" of the "children's bread" in order for her daughter to be healed. Jesus was impressed and moved by her response. He said, "Woman, you have great faith! Your request is granted."[7] And the woman's daughter was instantly healed.

When Jesus responded to the woman, the Old Covenant, the covenant God had established with Moses and the Israelites, was still in effect. And indeed, at this time, Gentiles were considered "dogs," the outcasts. This was the world Jesus stepped into when he entered humanity. But his death on the cross would totally change that paradigm. His death would be for all mankind, ushering in the New Covenant—a covenant with God no longer based on one's natural heritage. Being a child of God would no longer be dependent on one's natural birth, but rather on one's spiritual birth. The children of God would be those who receive Jesus, who believe on his name, *and* are born of God!

> Yet to all who did receive him to those who believed in his name, he gave the right to become the children of God —children *not of natural descent . . . but born of God.* (John 1:12)

---

[5] Matthew 15:23-28
[6] Matthew 15:27 NKJV
[7] Matthew 15:28

So we who look back to the cross have a spiritual identity not based on our nationality or ethnicity: it no longer matters where the lines of our physical heritage lead. As those who have accepted Jesus as our Savior, we are the children of God, and he has prepared daily bread for us. Not crumbs, but bread—the bread of healing and deliverance, the bread of comfort and peace, the bread of guidance and wisdom, the bread of hope and joy, the bread of an answered prayer. And we don't have to beg for it.

Begging is asking for what doesn't belong to you, what you have no right to receive. The bread prepared by the Father rightfully belongs to his children. And we who are his children only need to ask for it: "Father, *give us* this day our daily bread."[8]

Sermon on the Mount

In the Sermon on the Mount, Jesus again encourages us to ask for what the Father has prepared for us. Jesus delivered this sermon when his ministry was gaining momentum. Word of his powerful teaching and miraculous healings stirred hearts. They followed him from Galilee and the Decapolis, from Jerusalem and Judea, and the regions beyond the Jordan River. As a great crowd gathered, Jesus climbed up the side of the mountain, sat down and began teaching. They listened in amazement as he taught what we now refer to as the Beatitudes—the attitudes that bring blessing into our lives. He taught about loving our enemies, giving to the needy, praying and fasting, and storing up treasures in heaven. All topics worthy of a chapter of explanation in and of themselves. But toward the end of that sermon, Jesus gives us this instruction:

> "Keep on asking, and you will receive what you ask for. Keep on seeking, and you will find. Keep on knocking, and the door will be opened to you. For everyone who asks, receives. Everyone who seeks, finds. And to everyone who knocks, the door will be opened. You parents—if your children ask for a

---

[8] Matthew 6:11

loaf of bread, do you give them a stone instead? Or if they ask for a fish, do you give them a snake? Of course not! So if you sinful people know how to give good gifts to your children, how much more will your heavenly Father give good gifts to those who *ask* him?" (Matthew 7:7-11)

The Canaanite woman only asked for a crumb. And consider what just a crumb of the children's bread was able to do for her daughter. Just a crumb of the children's bread brought a miracle of healing. If that is what a *crumb* can do, consider what his *bread* can do for us—we who are now his children. Perhaps this is why we read in 1 Corinthians 2:9 (NLT), "No eye has seen, no ear has heard and no mind imagined what God has *prepared* for those who love him."

Lesson Two

We didn't earn it and we don't deserve it, but God made a way through the redemptive sacrifice of Jesus for our identity to be changed—to be adopted as a child of God with full rights of a begotten one. How wonderful, how marvelous, to be a child of God—not an outcast or outsider, not even just a friend or an acquaintance. No, his child! A child who is loved by God the Father with an extravagant love. One to whom Jesus said the Father desires to give good gifts, for whom he has prepared "daily bread." And Jesus encourages us to ask, to seek, to knock, believing for the good gifts he has for his children.

Chapter Challenge

- Thank the Lord that your adoption into his family is not dependent on your ethnicity or nationality, but rather on the One who is your Savior—Jesus Christ, his begotten Son.

- Embrace your adoption! As his child, ask your Heavenly Father for the "bread" you need today. Comfort? Healing? Guidance?

Provision? Patience? Forgiveness? Peace? Ask with confidence, for he is a loving Father who desires to supply all your needs.

- Ask the Lord to help you see yourself and others through the lens of being an adopted child of God. Allow the permanence and magnitude of God being your Heavenly Father to deepen your desire to live your life as a devoted follower of Christ.

Chapter 3

Embrace His Presence

He had big dreams. His future was laced with good fortune. He was destined to make a mark in this world. After all, he had been educated in Pharaoh's court, had grown up with wealth, privilege, and royal connections. But all his plans, all his hopes, had been dashed long ago.

As he had for most of the last forty years, Moses awoke to the bleating of sheep. All he could look forward to was another day of tending sheep, corralling them as they grazed. This day would be like all the rest. At least that was what he thought, until he saw something very strange. A bush was on fire, but it wasn't burning up. Curiosity got the best of him. With each step he took toward that strange bush, Moses drew closer to the moment when he would meet God and embark on a great journey. God would use Moses in a most significant way at a time when he felt most insignificant.

Moses' Childhood

To understand the deep insignificance and the utter despair Moses felt at this point in his life, consider the events surrounding his birth and childhood. He was born at a most ominous time—born into slavery, facing certain death. Due to the population explosion among the Israelites, the Egyptian pharaoh had decreed that all male Israelite infants were to be killed. Moses' mother could not bear to give up her son to certain death, so for three anxious months she hid him. Desperately searching for a way to spare her son's life, she fashioned a bold plan. She placed baby Moses in a water-proofed basket and set him among the reeds on the Nile River. Her hope was for someone in Pharaoh's household to see the child and save him. She assigned her daughter to follow along the riverbank as that precious basket floated down the river.

As God ordained it, the plan worked! Pharaoh's own daughter found Moses, adopted him as her child, and raised him in the house of Pharaoh. Moses grew up enjoying all the privileges of education, wealth, and social standing. At the age of forty, however, something happened to Moses. Although the Bible doesn't provide the details, we learn that Moses turned his back on his adopted identity as an Egyptian and embraced his true identity as an Israelite.

I imagine as Moses contemplated the miraculous circumstances of his life—spared from death, adopted into Pharaoh's family—he must certainly have believed he had been spared for a significant purpose. With all the knowledge and insight, with all the skills and connections he had acquired, surely he would have expected his destiny would be to deliver his true people, the Israelites, from the yoke of Egyptian slavery they had suffered under for 400 years. But one day this dream was dashed.

Moses came upon an Egyptian taskmaster abusing an Israelite, and the injustice incited Moses. In outrage, he killed the taskmaster. Believing that the murder had gone unnoticed, Moses quickly buried the Egyptian in the sand. His act, however, did not go unnoticed. The murder became common knowledge, not only to the Israelites but even to Pharaoh.

Fearing for his life, Moses fled to the Midian Desert, where he lived as a fugitive for the next forty years.[1] Instead of leading a purposeful life, his days were now filled with tending mindless sheep. All hope of being that great deliverer went up in smoke. Ashes!

---

[1] Exodus 2:15

The Burning Bush Experience

Over the next four decades, the prime years of his life, Moses lost his polish, his self-confidence, and his self-worth. Undoubtedly, he believed he had squandered any opportunity to do something significant. His only purpose now was to tend his father-in-law's sheep. But all that changed in one day with that strange bush. Curiosity drew him to the burning bush, but it was the *voice* he heard—a holy voice which spoke to him from that bush—that brought Moses to his knees. Humbled and in awe, Moses heard God give him this directive: "I am sending you to Pharaoh to bring my people the Israelites out of Egypt."[2] God was appointing Moses as the one he would use to deliver the Israelites from their bondage of slavery.

How do you imagine Moses responded? With excitement? With relief that his life would finally have purpose? With joy that what he had hoped to do forty years earlier would now become a reality? On the contrary. Basically, Moses told God that he had the wrong guy: "God, I tried to help my people when I was in my prime, and I failed miserably, so I certainly can't do it now. I've lost my abilities, my polish. I just can't do it." While Moses was insistent with his protest, God was persistent with his response, "I will be with you."[3] Forty years earlier, Moses had tried to deliver the Israelites and usher in justice with his own strength and abilities, and he had failed. The difference this time? God would be with him. And what a difference that would make!

When Moses was afraid no one would believe that God had appeared to him, God empowered him to use a staff to perform miraculous signs. When Moses felt he lacked the eloquence to speak before the new pharaoh, God assigned his brother Aaron as his spokesperson. Then God did for Moses what he hadn't even done for the founding fathers of Israel—Abraham, Isaac and Jacob—he

---

[2] Exodus 3:10
[3] Exodus 3:9-12 NKJV; Exodus 4:1-17

revealed his holy name. "This is what you are to say to the Israelites: 'I AM has sent me to you.'"[4]

Moses had an extraordinary meeting with God. But would he embrace God's presence by being obedient to God's call upon his life? Was he willing to allow God's presence—leading and guiding him—to transform his life? In spite of his initial reluctance and feelings of inferiority, Moses embraced this meeting with God, and we witness a powerful transformation of his life.

The Transformation

Moses, along with his brother Aaron, went to Pharaoh to deliver God's command to let the Israelites, God's people, go free. When Pharaoh refused, God sent plagues upon Egypt. There were plagues of flies that swarmed, frogs that filled their Egyptian homes, boils that covered their bodies, locusts that came like a great wind, consuming their crops. Despite these debilitating plagues, Pharaoh repeatedly refused to free the Israelites. After all, they were his labor force. Only after the tenth and final plague—death of the firstborn—as cries of grief and mourning filled the land of Egypt, did Pharaoh finally relent. No longer defying God's decree, Pharaoh released the Israelites. They were set free to leave the land of their bondage.

Why didn't God send the last plague first? Why bother with the frogs, the locusts, the flies? Why not go right to the plague of death? There is no question that God could have delivered the Israelites with just one plague. It wasn't as if God found it difficult to break down Pharaoh's resistance, and he needed to use ten plagues to do it. In fact, the Bible states that God intentionally hardened Pharaoh's heart. So why harden Pharaoh's heart? Why so many plagues?

The answer is, perhaps, two-fold. First of all, the plagues displayed in a most dramatic way the power of Almighty God—the power to decimate the economic and military might of the most powerful nation on earth. Each of the plagues defied one of Egypt's

---

[4] Exodus 3:14

many gods, showing both the Egyptians and the Israelites, not once but ten times, that it wasn't the gods of Egypt who possessed true power. Rather, it was the God of Abraham, Isaac, and Jacob who held the power. Up close and personal, both nations witnessed how God brought Egypt to its knees without a battle being fought or a sword being raised. The miracles of the plagues were to create faith in the Israelites to believe that what God had done for them in Egypt, he would continue to do as they journeyed to the Promised Land.

While God was revealing his faith-creating power to the Israelites, he was also doing something important in Moses' life. He was being transformed from a reluctant deliverer to a faith-filled leader. This man who once lacked the confidence to stand before Pharaoh was transformed into a man who confidently led over two million Israelites out of Egypt. As Moses faced the ongoing reluctance of Pharaoh, he learned a powerful lesson: to draw near to God and hear what God wanted him to do! With each plague that was visited upon Egypt, as Pharaoh vacillated with his responses, Moses learned to turn to God for direction, guidance, and wisdom. As he continued to embrace God's presence in his life, as his relationship with God deepened, his confidence grew.

When Pharaoh finally relented and allowed the Israelites to go free, Moses followed the travel instructions given to him by God, leading the people to the banks of the Red Sea. But Pharaoh once again changed his mind and was determined to exact revenge. When the Israelites realized the Egyptian army was in hot pursuit, they cried out in fear. But not Moses! With great boldness and confidence in God, Moses extended his rod, believing God would miraculously part the waters of the Red Sea so the people could cross safely to the other side. The Moses who extended his rod to part the Red Sea as a massive Egyptian army is in sight is a far cry from the broken, disillusioned, purposeless man whom God met at the burning bush.

There is no doubt Moses' burning bush experience with God was life-changing, but it didn't instantly mature him. It wasn't the fulfillment of his destiny but rather an encounter with God that set him *on the journey* to fulfill his destiny. At the burning bush, Moses *began* his journey of transformation to become the "who" God had purposed him to be—a great leader—instead of the "who" Moses thought he was—a failure. His journey with God began with a spiritual experience, but Moses was transformed into a great man of faith by learning to *draw near to God*. He learned *to hear and to do* as he embraced God's presence.

The Mountain Meeting

Moses had a burning bush experience, but the Israelites were going to have a Mt. Sinai experience! After leaving Egypt and walking through the Red Sea on dry ground, Moses was instructed by God to lead the Israelites to Mt. Sinai. That is where God would meet them. This is where God would make a covenant with them. His covenant promise was to transform the Israelites into a holy nation, a royal priesthood, a special treasure unto God. How wonderful it must have been for these Israelite slaves, who had labored under prejudice, ridicule, and injustice for centuries, to hear such a promise. A holy nation! A royal priesthood! A special treasure! Almost too good to be true. However, this covenant promise was contingent on their choice to follow God, to listen to his voice and obey his instructions—*to hear and to do!* The Israelites emphatically declared that they would be obedient and do all that God required.

As instructed, the Israelites stood at the base of Mt. Sinai. The time had come for God to reveal himself to them. The mountain top was covered with a dark cloud. They saw God's power as lightning stuck with great rolls of thunder. They felt God's power as the mountain began to quake. They heard great trumpet blasts. Then they watched as the presence of God came down upon the mountain as a great fire. Through the thunder and the trumpet blasts, they heard the voice of God speak to them—proclaiming the Ten Commandments.[5]

What a tremendous meeting with God! Imagine if we could see God's power, feel his might, then hear his voice as the Israelites did. What an awe-inspiring, faith-producing experience that would be.

---

[5] Exodus 19:5-8 NKJV; Deuteronomy 5:6-22

Surely if we had that kind of meeting with God, our faith walk would be set for life. No problem, no adversity, nothing that life could throw our way would keep us from following God. Nothing would keep us from fulfilling God's plan and purpose for our lives. Right? You would think so. But we read something astonishing that took place not long after the Israelites' mountain meeting with God.

They Stood Afar Off

Moses was called up into the mountain so God could give him the Ten Commandments written on stone tablets, as well as the judicial and religious laws to establish the Israelites as a nation. Back at camp, the people waited. One week, two weeks, three weeks—a month passed. Moses still had not returned from the mountain top.[6] Uncertain if Moses would ever return, the people began to murmur, and this is where the story takes a bewildering turn.

They gathered around Aaron and made this demand: make us a "god," an idol, who will lead us out of this wilderness. So using their Egyptian gold jewelry, Aaron molded a golden calf. Then the people worshiped that idol saying, "This is the god who brought us out of Egypt!" And they engaged in pagan worship rituals. How could they attribute to a handmade idol the great miracles of deliverance performed by God Almighty, the *living* God? It had only been a month since they met God, experiencing firsthand his power. They had even heard God speak! How could they revert so quickly to the idolatry of Egypt? How could this have happened?

The answer lies in the Israelites' response after their mountain meeting with God. They told Moses, "You speak to us and we'll listen, but don't have God speak to us or we'll die." Now they had heard God speak, and they were still living. Nevertheless, fear gripped them. Moses quickly responded by encouraging them not to be afraid. He explained that God had shown them his fearsome power so they would be motivated to obey God and not sin. But Moses' words fell on deaf ears. They could not be persuaded. "*So the*

---

[6] Exodus 32:1-6

people stood afar off, but Moses drew near to the thick darkness where God was."[7]

The response of the Israelites to their mountain meeting with God was a choice to keep him at arm's length, to know God only through Moses—a second-hand relationship. This arrangement worked fine until uncertainty entered the picture, until adversity raised its head. And when it did, this generation of Israelites had a persistent habit of throwing up their hands in despair, bemoaning their deliverance from Egypt, quickly abandoning their faith and disobeying God. This habit was first apparent at Mt. Sinai, when they were uncertain if Moses would return from the mountain, but was continually displayed throughout their journey to the Promised Land. In fact, this generation of Israelites never became the people God desired them to be. Theirs was a legacy of immature faith, because after meeting God they made a fateful choice to keep God at a distance in their lives: "They stood afar off." They failed to embrace his presence.

A Starting Point

Maybe you have not had as dramatic a meeting with God as Moses did at a burning bush or the Israelites did at Mt. Sinai, but you have met the Lord. He has touched your life. Maybe it was in a response to an altar call at church, or at a youth meeting, or in the solitude of your own home. You know with great certainty that Jesus is your Savior, but just like Moses and the Israelites, your initial experience with God isn't meant to be the climax of your spiritual journey. No, it's but the beginning!

Once you have met the Lord, once you have accepted Jesus as your Savior, it is essential that you choose to draw near to him, so you can *hear* him and then *do* what he says. This is how you, like Moses, are transformed! You need a personal, individual relationship with God; this is his desire. Not to be known through the faith of your mother or father, your husband or wife, your pastor or teacher

---

[7] Exodus 20:19 NKJV

or friend. Not to be known second-hand! If you make the choice to know God through someone else's faith, to keep God at a distance in your life, then when you face adversity, when things don't go the way you expect, then you, like the Israelites, will find yourself reverting to the disobedient habits of your "Egypt"—a consequence of immature faith. And you will miss out on the transformative, intimate presence of God in your life.

In Chapter 1, I shared the story of my older sister who suffers from Alzheimer's. As I reflect upon the grace with which she faced this devastating disease, I know it was rooted in her close relationship with Jesus. As a teenager in a youth meeting, she had made a choice not to rely on the faith of my parents but to engage in a personal relationship with Jesus. As that relationship deepened, as she made the choice to draw near to him, she was *transformed* into a woman of great faith. So, when Alzheimer's became a reality in her life, her faith became her anchor. Certainly there were tears and questions, but my sister never blamed God. She didn't shake her fist at him and demand to know why she wasn't being healed—why there was no miracle for her. She didn't whine and complain to him. She didn't turn her *back on God*; instead, she turned *to him* for comfort. And she knew how to do that, because for over fifty years she had made the choice to draw near to the Lord. She knew how to draw strength from her intimate relationship with Jesus to face a disease that would be unbearable for her to face alone. She had made the choice to embrace his presence.

Surely the apostle James understood this truth as well, for he was inspired to declare the promise: "Draw near to God and he will draw near to you." (James 4:8) We read this verse and it inspires us, but how do we apply it to our lives? How do we draw near to God when there is no burning bush to approach, no Mt. Sinai to climb?

Lesson Three

We draw near to God by devoting ourselves to studying God's Word and applying its truths to our lives—by doing them. *We embrace his presence* by taking time to pray and praise God, not just in a church service or in a small group meeting, but alone in a private place of prayer. Through devotion to God's Word and prayer, we express our desire to personally know the God who already knows us and to be transformed by him. If we, like Moses, choose to draw near to God, to *hear* and *do* what he says, he will transform the brokenness of our lives. He will remove our lack of confidence and feelings of unworthiness. He will replace hopelessness with hope, disillusionment with a vision for the future. Where we are weak, he will make us strong. He will reveal his divine destiny and plan for our lives. But it is our choice: to stand afar off by keeping God at arm's length in our lives, or to draw near to the Lord, embracing his presence by engaging in a personal relationship with him.

Chapter Challenge

- Evaluate your relationship with the Lord:
  - Have you kept him at arm's length in your life? Do you rely on the faith others have in Jesus instead of drawing near to him for yourself? Do you go to others first to ask for prayer regarding a need or situation in your life, instead of bringing that need to the Lord yourself?
  - Did you once have a close relationship with Jesus, but the distractions and disappointments of life have caused you to distant yourself from him?

- Find a quiet place to pray and with total sincerity tell Jesus that you desire an intimate, vibrant relationship with him—a relationship that will transform you into the "who" he has purposed you to be. Embrace his presence as he responds to your heartfelt prayer.

Chapter 4

Embrace His Expectation

Quietly I would creep up the stairs to my sister's lone bedroom on the third floor to sit on the end of her bed so that I could watch her study. She was nineteen and attended something magical called college. I was nine and simply went to elementary school. Her classes were intriguing—World Lit, Calculus, Ancient Civilization. My classes were mundane—reading, writing, and arithmetic. Her world was filled with dances, dates, and cruising. My world was riding bikes and playing Jacks. She was blond and beautiful; I wore glasses and had braces. As I sat on that bed, I wanted to grow up to be just like my big sister.

My sister is pretty incredible and one who deserves to be emulated, but she is by no means perfect. The idea of growing up to be like her seemed lofty, yet attainable. But consider for a moment the expectation that God has for us, one that would seem unattainable. We, the Father's adopted ones, are to emulate his only Son, our big brother, Jesus.

> For God knew his people in advance, and he chose them to *become like his Son,* so that his Son would be the firstborn among many brothers and sisters. (Romans 8:29)

There is no question that Jesus is worthy of our emulation. When we read about his life and ministry, we see a profound intimacy with the Father and an unwavering obedience to him. Jesus displays a genuine heart of love and compassion to save the lost, heal the sick, deliver the oppressed. His wisdom surpassed King Solomon's. His love for the

Word exceeded King David's. His power to perform miracles was greater than the great prophets'. Yes, Jesus is worthy of our emulation, but how daunting is this expectation of the Father—to become like Jesus? Yet Ephesians 5 confirms this expectation:

> Imitate God, therefore, in everything you do, because you are his dear children. Live a life filled with love, *following the example of Christ.* (Ephesians 5:1-2 NLT)

Become like Christ. Follow his example. Imitate him in everything we do. Daunting is an understatement! But God knows our limitations: He knows we cannot become more like Jesus, become Christ-like, on our own strength. So he sent us a helper—the Holy Spirit.

The Helper

The hours were passing too quickly, the minutes flying by swiftly. This was the last night Jesus would spend with his disciples before his crucifixion. And as he sat down with the disciples sharing this last supper, there was a noticeable change in Jesus. Like a parent giving last-minute instructions to his children before departing on a long journey, there was an urgency in Jesus' instructions—an urgency mixed with great compassion.

Jesus was preparing them for what would take place in the hours ahead, and they didn't like what they were hearing. They didn't want Jesus to leave them. They didn't want things to change. Sorrow and grief filled their hearts. These last three years with Jesus had been incredible—amazing miracles of healings and deliverance, even the dead being brought back to life. Then there were the remarkable teachings: the Sermon on the Mount, the parables that stymied even the most astute religious Pharisees and Sadducees. But best of all were the intimate conversations, the personal revelations of truth Jesus shared with them. So it was with great compassion that Jesus assured his disciples it was in their best interest that his ministry as they knew it was coming to an end. Jesus declared:

> "Nevertheless I tell you the truth. It is to your advantage that I go away; for if I do not go away, the Helper (*the Holy Spirit*) will not come to you; but if I depart, I will send Him to you."
> (John 16:7 NKJV)

How could having the Holy Spirit be better than having Jesus right there with them? Jesus explained the advantage: the Holy Spirit would not just be with them, but would dwell *in* them. They would be empowered from within: ". . . you know him, for he (the Holy Spirit) lives with you and will be *in* you."[1] That night the disciples didn't understand the advantage of having the Holy Spirit at work *within* them, but on the day of Pentecost that changed. After Jesus' resurrection, moments before he ascended into heaven, Jesus delivered these final instructions:

> "And now I will send the Holy Spirit, just as my Father promised. But stay here in the city (Jerusalem) until the Holy Spirit comes and fills you with *power* from heaven."
> (Luke 24:49 NLT)

So the disciples obeyed. They waited in Jerusalem. On the Day of Pentecost, fifty days after Jesus' resurrection, they were filled with the promised Holy Spirit, their Helper. Empowered from within, the change in the disciples was apparent, especially in Peter. Weeks earlier, on the night Jesus was apprehended by the Jewish leaders, Peter, fearful for his own life, had blatantly denied Jesus three times and disavowed any association with him. This was the same disciple who, earlier that same evening, had emphatically declared to Jesus that though the other disciples might run for their lives, he would always remain faithful.

Peter was certain he would never deny Jesus. Yet when his own life was in jeopardy, he did what he had vowed he wouldn't do. He denied ever knowing Christ. But now, after being filled with the Holy Spirit and empowered from within, Peter stood before thousands and boldly preached the good news: salvation through Jesus Christ. In the years that followed, even when faced with imprisonment and death, Peter never backed down from preaching about Jesus. Peter's fear had been replaced

---

[1] John 14:17

with an inspired boldness. He possessed a strength of character like never before. Empowered by the Holy Spirit, Peter became one of the prominent leaders of the early church.

The Holy Spirit is a great Helper. And just as he influenced and empowered the lives of those first-century disciples, he can do the same for us today. The Holy Spirit will be our Helper. He can embolden our faith and empower us to fulfill God's purpose for our lives. The Holy Spirt will help us embrace the Father's expectation that we, who are his adopted children, become like his only begotten Son, Jesus. Help we absolutely need!

We need the Holy Spirit at work in our lives. We need his influence to change our desires and the behaviors of our sin-inclined nature—that innate part of us that has a natural bent toward self-centeredness, disobedience, and rebellion; that instinctive pull within us to do what is wrong rather than what is right; that instinctive desire to want our own way. We need the advantage that Jesus promised: to have the empowering Holy Spirit at work in our lives producing Christ-like changes, what the Scriptures refer to as "fruit."

The Importance of Fruit

Every year, my husband and I love to take road trips in our home state of Michigan, especially trips that take us along the coast of Lake Michigan. As you travel north and drive over the rolling hills, not only do you take in the beauty of this Great Lake but also the amazing patchwork of orchards—miles and miles of fruit trees planted in straight rows. By late summer or early fall, the spring blossoms have given way to abundant fruit hanging among the leaves on the trees. So by fall, even if you aren't an experienced farmer or a knowledgeable horticulturist, you can easily determine what kind of tree is in each orchard by its fruit. When you see cherries hanging from the tree, you know it's a cherry tree. The same for apples, pears, and peaches. The fruit identifies the tree.

This truth in nature can be applied to our lives spiritually. The Lord wants the people we live with, work with, go to church with, and come in contact with each day to know what "tree" we are by our "fruit." People should know that we are Christians by what we say and do. By how we act and react. By the way we authentically live our faith. Perhaps this is why the apostle Paul was inspired to define the "fruit" we are to bear as Christians, as Christ-followers— children of God:

> . . . let the Holy Spirit guide your lives. Then you won't be doing what your sinful nature craves. The sinful nature wants to do evil, which is just the opposite of what the Spirit wants. And the Spirit *gives us desires* that are the opposite of what the sinful nature desires. . . .*the Holy Spirit produces this kind of fruit in our lives*: love, joy, peace, patience, kindness, goodness, faithfulness, gentleness, and self-control. (Galatians 5:16-17, 22-23 NLT)

These fruits of the Spirit are the Christ-like qualities that are to be evident in our daily lives. It's the kind of fruit the presence of the Holy Spirit *at work within us* produces. Yet note that Paul's exhortation begins with the choice to *let* the Holy Spirit guide our lives.

The Holy Spirit can be a powerful agent of change in our lives if we let him. And when we do, he changes the desires of our heart and strengthens our will to make the choice of change. For you see, we are not passive in this change process. The maturing and perfecting of our character requires us to be active participants in partnership with the Holy Spirit. We will not attain perfection in this lifetime, but certainly the Lord wants us to be engaged in the perfecting process on this side of heaven, the process of "becoming like Christ." Consider Paul's instructions to the church in Ephesus:

> Since you have heard about Jesus and have learned the truth that comes from him, *throw off* your old sinful nature and your former way of life. . . Instead, *let* the Spirit renew your thoughts and attitudes. *Put on* your new nature, created to be like God— truly righteous and holy. (Ephesians 4:21-24 NLT)

Note the key verbs in this passage, a call to action:

> We are *to throw off* the old habits.
> We are *to let* the Spirit renew our minds.
> We are *to put on* the nature of Christ.

The Holy Spirit reveals to us what needs to be changed in our lives, creates in us the desire to change, and empowers us to make that change. But ultimately, we must make the active choice to change—to put off the habits of our sinful nature and to put on the character of Christ. We must choose to replace hatred with love, worry with peace, impatience with patience, and the desire for revenge with forgiveness. We must choose to replace cruelty with kindness, evil with good, disloyalty with faithfulness, harshness with gentleness. We must choose to replace destructive, excessive behavior with self-control, disobedience with obedience, and dishonesty with truth. The Holy Spirit empowers, but we act upon his empowerment with the *choice* to change. And as we make that choice, day by day, month by month, year by year, we become more like Christ, our big brother. For a moment, though, let's look back at an event in the life of Jesus, where at first glance his own actions seem un-Christlike.

In and Out of Season

Jesus and his twelve disciples had spent the night in Bethany, a small village on the outskirts of Jerusalem. Rising early the next morning, they started on their two-mile hike to Jerusalem. Not far from Bethany, Jesus, being hungry, looked for something to eat. He went up to a fig tree by the side of the road. "When he reached it, he found nothing but leaves, because it was not the season for figs."[2] Then Jesus did something bewildering: He cursed the tree! He declared, "May no one ever eat fruit from you again."[3] The next day, as they left Bethany to return to Jerusalem, the disciples noticed the fig tree was withered and dead.

This scene bothered me for a long time. Why would Jesus curse this tree? It seemed totally out of character, more like that of a petulant child than the Son of God. Jesus was upset with the fig tree because it was not bearing fruit. But clearly the Scriptures state it wasn't the season for figs. Why did Jesus even check for figs when he knew they were out of season? And if he knew they were out of season, why curse the tree? If it had been the season for figs, his displeasure would be understandable.

---

[2] Mark 11:13
[3] Mark 11:14

Through the example of the fig tree, one lesson among many is that of expectations. There is an expectation for God's children to bear the fruit of Christ's character not just when it is "in season," but also when it is "out of season." In season—when things are going great in our lives, and out of season—when we are facing life's struggles. "Out- of-season" fruit looks like this:

> *When we face financial difficulties, we still give.*
> *When we are faced with vindictiveness, we still forgive.*
> *When we are passed over for a promotion,*
> *we still work with excellence.*
> *We show compassion to those who show us none.*
> *We are obedient even when it is not an easy choice.*

In the Sermon on the Mount, Jesus provides examples of "out-of-season" fruit when he gives us this command:

> "Love your enemies, bless those who curse you, do good to those who hate you, and pray for those who spitefully use you and persecute you . . ." (Matthew 5:44 NKJV)

Just as Jesus looked for figs among the leaves, the Father is looking for the "out-of-season fruit" in our lives. And when he finds that kind fruit in us, Jesus is pleased.

> In this way, you will be acting as true children of your Father in heaven. . . . If you love only those who love you, what reward is there for that? Even corrupt tax collectors do that much. If you are kind only to your friends, how are you different from anyone else? . . . (Matthew 5:45-48 NLT)

In the Message Bible translation, Jesus summed it up this way: "Live out your God-created identity." So how do we do that? How do we work in partnership with the Holy Spirit to produce that "in- and out-of-season" fruit? How do we allow him to influence our lives, so that we make the choice of change that bears the fruit the Father is seeking—the Father expects? We allow the Holy Spirit to be our teacher. These words

47

Jesus spoke to his disciples are still true for us today: "But the Helper, the Holy Spirit, whom the Father will send in My name, He will teach you all things. . . "[4] The Holy Spirit uses the Bible to teach us. He uses these inspired words of God penned in ancient times to inspire us today to bear the fruit of change in our lives. Paul, in writing to his mentee Timothy, explains this concerning the Bible:

> All scripture is inspired by God and is useful to teach us what is true and to make us realize what is wrong in our lives. It corrects us when we are wrong and teaches us to do what is right. God uses it to prepare and equip his people to do every good work. (2 Timothy 3:16-17 NLT)

The Sower and The Seed

In yet another of Jesus' powerful sermons, he tells the parable of the Sower and the Seed. A primary lesson of this story focuses on evangelism, and how the Word of God can be received and responded to in different ways. But there's also a lesson here instructing us to embrace the Word of God as the Holy Spirit makes it alive to us, which leads to bearing the fruit of Christ-like qualities.

As the crowd pressed in on the Sea of Galilee to hear Jesus preach, he climbed aboard an offshore boat and used it as his pulpit. His sermon stirred the hearts of the people as he spoke about a farmer planting seed. Some of the farmer's seed fell on a hard path, and the birds quickly snatched it up. Jesus explained to his disciples that this represents people who hear God's Word, but their hearts are hard and the Word never takes root.

Then there was seed that fell on rocky places where there wasn't much soil. The seed took root, but when the hot sun came out, the plants were scorched and quickly withered. This represents people who hear God's Word and are initially inspired by it, but their passion is short-lived.

---

[4] John 14:26 NKJV

"But there is such shallow soil of character that when the emotions wear off and some difficulty arrives, there is nothing to show for it." (Mark 4:17 MSG)

No fruit.

Next there was the seed planted in soil among weeds and thorns. The seed took root and the plants grew, but they never produced any fruit because they were choked out by weeds and thorns. Jesus explained,

"The seed that fell among the thorns represents others who hear God's word, but all too quickly the message is crowded out by the worries of this life, the lure of wealth, and the desire for other things, so no fruit is produced." (Mark 4:18 NLT)

Indeed, the weeds of life—our worries, the lure of wealth, and the desire for other things—can sap our energy and divert our focus. These weeds choke out spiritual life and strength, causing us to respond with impatience instead of patience, anger instead of love, covetousness instead of generosity, harsh criticism instead of forgiveness and gentleness. But remember Jesus sent us a Helper, the Holy Spirit. So when we are bombarded by the worries of life, the Holy Spirit at work within us can be our Comforter who can calm our fears and relieve our worries. He reminds us that God never forsakes the righteous—that our heavenly Father has daily bread for us. He is the supplier of all our needs. He loves and cherishes his children, so he will take care of us.

When it comes to the lure of wealth and the desire for other things, the Holy Spirit reminds us that "life does not consist in the abundance of things." [5] He teaches us to focus on seeking after the kingdom of God—his righteousness, his peace, and his joy. Then all of the *things* will be given to us as well. [6] When the good things of life are added to our lives as blessings, then our possessions don't possess us. They won't become strangling weeds or thorns.

---

[5] Luke 12:15
[6] Matthew 6:33

This parable concludes with seed being planted in good soil, which produced a plentiful harvest—thirty, sixty, even a hundred times as much as was planted. Jesus explains,

> "The seed planted in the good earth represents those who hear the Word, *embrace it*, and produce a harvest beyond their wildest dreams." (Mark 4:20 MSG)

They produce much fruit, much "in- and out-of-season" fruit.

In this parable, there were four ways in which the seed was planted, but it was always the same seed, the Word of God. In each instance, the Word was heard, whether it was sown on hard soil, rocky soil, among the weeds, or in good soil. However, it was only in the good soil that *much* fruit was produced. Why? Because the Word was not only heard, the Word was *embraced.* The *embracing* of the Word is what made the difference, yet this is where the challenge lies.

How often do we hear or read a passage of scripture, and our hearts are pricked, yet we deflect the conviction? Or perhaps we hesitate to embrace the Word because we make excuses for why it doesn't apply to us, or we just talk ourselves out of the urgency to act upon it. Sometimes God's Word is uncomfortable because it requires difficult change. Yet when that Word challenges us, when it pricks our heart, or quickens our conscience, the Holy Spirit is helping us—revealing what needs to change, what actions to take, what attitudes need adjusting.

This is how the Holy Spirit helps us change our desires: He empowers our will to make the choice to change as he makes God's words come alive. This is how we embrace the Father's expectation to follow Christ's example and imitate him in everything we do.

Lesson Four

Just as Jesus searched among the leaves of that fig tree for fruit, God is searching our hearts to see if the character of Christ is being formed in us. And when we begin to live out our God-created identities as his children, when our lives emulate the character of our big brother, Jesus

Christ, when we begin to bear "in- and out-of-season" fruit, our lives glorify God the Father. Embrace these words of Jesus: "When you produce *much* fruit, you are my true disciples. (And) this brings great glory to my Father."[7]

Chapter Challenge

- Do not be overwhelmed by the Father's expectation to become Christ-like. Instead, thank God for the Holy Spirit and express your desire to embrace him as your teacher.

- Make a plan to read the Bible regularly. Choose a translation that is reader-friendly, such as the New International Version or the New Living Translation. There are numerous translations, but these two are a great place to start. Bible Gateway, an online resource, offers a variety of Bible reading plans.(www.biblegateway.com/reading-plans)

- Ask the Holy Spirit to make the Scriptures you read come alive, so that you will become more sensitive to his direction for your life and empowered by his leading to make the changes in your attitudes and actions that will empower you to bear much fruit, in- and out-of-season.

- What "in-season" fruit is evident in your life today? What "out-of-season" fruit is lacking? Express your desire to God to be recognized as a child of God who is known by your Christ-like fruit.

---

[7] John 15:8

Chapter 5

Embrace His Plan

In the opening pages of this book I described my reluctance as a volunteer on an outreach team who prayed with inmates after an evangelist gave her testimony of healing and deliverance. But I need to add that when I entered the prison that day, my intention was for it to be a one-time experience. Prison ministry had never been something I was drawn to or ever felt God wanted me to pursue. Some Christians feel the call to be a pastor or a missionary, while others are drawn to work with the elderly or the homeless. I knew God had called me to be a teacher, had given me a passion to teach, and had provided numerous opportunities to teach his Word, not only in my church but also at conferences and retreats. But prison ministry? Not an inkling! No desire at all.

After meeting and praying with those inmates, though, God birthed an unexpected plan in my heart. As our team debriefed, we all agreed that these men needed something more than prayer. They needed to be taught. They needed a course of study that would ground them in the Word of God and provide them with a solid spiritual foundation. It was no coincidence that for over 20 years I had been involved in teaching a course called "Understanding God," from an identically titled text written by my mother-in-law, Patricia Beall Gruits. I had been involved in edits of the text, and wrote a leader's guide and a student workbook to accompany it. I had taught hundreds of people over the years. I had even partnered with my mother-in-law in conducting seminars to assist pastors and church leaders around the country to implement this Bible study in their churches. The "Understanding God" study had gained great recognition in anchoring and strengthening the faith of believers, whether they were seekers or seasoned Christians.

As we talked about how moved we were by the needs of these inmates and their hunger to grow in their faith, I found myself voicing this compelling thought: "I think we should try to teach the 'Understanding God' class here at the prison." As soon as the words tumbled out of my mouth, I wanted to suck them back in. Inside there was a voice exclaiming, "Joy, what in the world are you saying? Now that you put it out there, you are going to have to do something! This was supposed to be a one-time experience. One and done! What are you getting yourself into?" But deep in my heart, I knew this was why God had brought me to the event. Even though I recognized that teaching this class in a maximum-security prison would be way outside of my comfort zone, I knew this was part of God's plan for my life. But I now faced a difficult choice. Would I go where God was leading me?

It would mean a long drive every week. It would mean going to a scary, intimidating place: stark walls, worn chairs, a smell of hundreds of men in confined spaces. A world so foreign from my own. I'll be honest, there was a huge part of me that hoped my efforts to teach this class in prison would fall through. Perhaps the chaplain would not be open to such a class. Perhaps prison rules would not allow a woman to teach at a men's prison.

But this was God's plan, not mine. The friend who had invited me knew the regional director of Prison Fellowship, an organization founded by Chuck Colson. She arranged a meeting with the new chaplain at the prison. He was impressed with the vision and gave me permission to teach this foundation course for the next two years.

Teaching in a maximum-security prison was an experience I never thought God would ask of me. Prison was the last place I ever expected I would use the gift of teaching God had given me. My plan was just to teach in a church environment. But in those two years, stereotypes were shattered, and I saw God's hand in his plan for me to teach these men—broken children of God whom he wanted to restore. Men who were eager to be followers of Christ!

Although God's plan for my life involved going to a prison to teach, God's plan for one of the great patriarchs of the Bible was to be enslaved and thrown into prison. Let's look at the lessons we can learn from Joseph and how he responded to God's unexpected plan for his life.

Unexpected Plan

Joseph's life began auspiciously. He was the favored son of his father, Jacob. He had eleven brothers, ten of them older, and Joseph definitely was the apple of his father's eye. Every time he wore his ornate coat, a special gift from his father, his brothers were reminded of Joseph's favored status. Every time he was shown preferential treatment by Jacob, their resentment intensified. And when Joseph shared the dreams he had at night—dreams that placed him in a position of power and authority over his brothers and even his father—their resentment turned into hatred.

One day, Jacob sent Joseph to gather a report on the brothers' management of the family business—tending sheep. This assignment was not unusual for Joseph. At seventeen, instead of joining his brothers as a shepherd, he was his father's eyes and ears. Again, preferential treatment. So Joseph left Canaan and traveled to Dothan. When his brothers saw him approaching, their hatred birthed a plan of murder. Upon Joseph's arrival, their jealous hands stripped him of his embroidered coat. They threw him into a dry cistern and left him to die in this wilderness pit, with no hope of escape.

Joseph, bewildered and confused, desperately cried out to his brothers for help. But they refused to respond to his plea. With heartbreak, then hopelessness, he realized how much his brothers hated him. Their deep-seated jealousy had turned into a deep-seated hatred. That evening as the brothers sat down to eat their evening meal, they saw in the distance a caravan of Midianite traders coming their way. Having a slight change of heart, the brothers altered their plan. They would sell Joseph to the Midianites, who in turn would sell him into Egyptian slavery. Spared from death, Joseph now faced an uncertain future as a slave.

As Joseph was placed in shackles, and with every step that brought him closer to Egypt, he was overcome with fear and despair. Everything and everyone he knew and loved was gone. No hope ever again to bask in his father's love. As he stood on that auction block, as he listened to his life being sold to a man in a land that was foreign in language and culture, every thought must have screamed, "God, this isn't supposed to be the plan for my life!" But it *was* God's plan. Joseph just didn't know the details of that plan. God was going to use the next few years to teach him obedience and trust. He had to learn to be *obedient* in the present as God led him to his future. He had to *trust* that he was part of God's greater plan.

Obedience in the Present

Joseph was sold to Potiphar, an Egyptian captain of Pharaoh's palace guard. As a slave, Joseph was severed from the love and favor of his father, Jacob, but not from the love and favor of his heavenly Father. Whatever Joseph put his hand to was blessed. Whatever task he was assigned went well. God's favor upon Joseph was so apparent that even an idol-worshiper like Potiphar recognized it and advanced Joseph to the position of his personal assistant. When it came to bills being paid, investments being made, business affairs being managed, all aspects of Potiphar's household were administered by Joseph. In fact, the Bible states that Potiphar had no concerns about anything except the food he ate."[1] Joseph wasn't living in the land of his choice. He wasn't with the people he loved. Yet, whatever task he was assigned he met it with energy and excellence, with no hint of resentment or bitterness. Joseph had been horribly wronged, but he didn't let the wrong permeate his spirit. As Potiphar's household

---

[1] Genesis 39:6

manager, Joseph gained knowledge and skills in finance and business management he would never have gained as a shepherd in Canaan.

Joseph recognized God's favor was upon him. What he didn't recognize was that everything he was learning in Potiphar's house was an important and necessary detail in the next step of God's plan for his life. The end of God's plan was still not in Joseph's sight. It was impossible for him to see where God was ultimately leading him, especially when his time in Potiphar's house came to an abrupt and disheartening end.

Potiphar's Wife

In Potiphar's house, Joseph had achieved a level of security and comfort. He had adjusted to his status as a favored servant. Overall, things were going well, with one exception—the repeated advances by Potiphar's wife. Frustrated by her failed attempts to seduce Joseph, she turned on him with false accusations. Believing her lies, Potiphar threw Joseph into the palace prison.

No longer an honored servant, Joseph was now an enslaved prisoner. Once again he faced an uncertain future. Surely Joseph must have cried out to God in bewilderment: "I didn't do anything wrong. I did everything right, yet I end up in prison? God, how can this be part of your plan?" Joseph may have been bewildered by his circumstance, but his faith in God never wavered. His awareness that God was with him never waned. Even in prison, God's favor was evident.

> But the Lord was with Joseph in the prison and showed him his faithful love. And the Lord made Joseph a favorite with the prison warden. Before long the warden put Joseph in charge of all the other prisoners and over everything that happened in the prison. The warden had no worries, because Joseph took care of everything. The Lord was with him and caused everything he did to succeed.
> (Genesis 39: 21-23 NLT)

In Potiphar's house, Joseph learned how to manage household affairs. In prison, he learned how to administer the business affairs of an entire institution. He managed budgets, schedules, and even the inmates. Although a prisoner himself, Joseph embraced the opportunity to be productive and expand his knowledge and abilities, just as he had done in Potiphar's house.

No matter how difficult or discouraging his circumstances, his attitude remained positive and his work ethic never diminished. In prison, Joseph gained a greater confidence in his business management skills, but he also matured spiritually as his gift to interpret dreams was fine-tuned.

The Baker and the Cupbearer

Due to Pharaoh's displeasure with both his baker and cupbearer, he sent them to the palace prison. One night both men had perplexing and worrisome dreams. The following morning, as Joseph carried out his administrative duties, he noticed something was wrong. Something was causing these men deep distress. Without hesitation, they shared their unsettling dreams with Joseph. As they did, God gave Joseph the interpretations to their dreams. And three days later, they proved true. The baker was executed but the cupbearer was freed. As the cupbearer left prison, out of gratitude to Joseph he promised to plead Joseph's case before Pharaoh. (You can read the whole story in Genesis 40 and 41.)

Joseph's faith in God must have been strengthened, and his expectation for imminent deliverance from prison seemed certain. But Joseph's release was not the next detail in God's plan. As soon as the cupbearer was reinstated, he forgot about Joseph. There was no release. There was no pardon. Why would God give Joseph the interpretation of these dreams to men who had direct access to Pharaoh if God wasn't going to use this miracle to bring deliverance for Joseph? That would have been my expectation, and certainly Joseph's as well.

Yet there is no record of Joseph's complaint or disillusionment. No questions being asked. No change in his attitude or work ethic. No change in his commitment to God. Joseph could have thrown up his hands in despair. But he didn't. .Even though Joseph didn't understand why he was still in prison, even though he saw no end in sight, he continued to have faith in God. He believed that somehow, someway, even being in prison was a necessary part of God's plan for his life. Joseph would patiently wait for God's purpose to be revealed.

From Prison to the Palace

Two more years had passed since Joseph had interpreted the cupbearer's dream, when Pharaoh had two disturbing dreams of his own. None of his magicians or wise men could decipher them. Now, finally, the cupbearer remembered Joseph and relayed to Pharaoh that Joseph possessed a gift to accurately interpret dreams. With great urgency, Pharaoh sent for him. Quickly made presentable, Joseph stood before Pharaoh, who implored him to interpret the dreams.

> "It is beyond my power to do this," Joseph replied. "But God can tell you what it means and set you at ease." (Genesis 41:16 NLT)

And God did. He gave Joseph the interpretation of the two dreams: one foretelling seven years of prosperity, the other foretelling seven following years of famine. Then he outlined an economic plan for how to use the years of prosperity to survive and prosper during the years of famine. Pharaoh was so impressed with Joseph and his plan that he made the following decree:

> "Can we find anyone else like this man so obviously filled with the spirit of God? . . . Since God has revealed the meaning of the dreams to you, clearly no one else is as intelligent or wise as you are. You will be in charge of my court, and all my people will take orders from you. Only I, sitting on my throne, will have a rank higher than yours." (Genesis 41:37-40 NLT)

In a matter of one day, Joseph was elevated from prisoner to second-in-command over the land of Egypt. And Joseph met the challenge of this enormous task with great success. But where did he get the confidence to interpret Pharaoh's dreams without fear or hesitation? It came from his experience of having divinely inspired dreams as a teen. It came from his experience in prison, interpreting the dreams of Pharaoh's baker and cupbearer. Where did Joseph gain the knowledge and skill to manage the economic affairs of Egypt? It came from his experience as a slave managing the affairs in Potiphar's house and as a prisoner administering the affairs of the palace prison. As a slave and then a prisoner, Joseph acquired the necessary skills and knowledge to become the governor of Egypt.

But more importantly, it was during these difficult years he learned to engage in his relationship with God, continually turning to him for strength and wisdom. These years were a necessary part of God's ultimate plan for Joseph's life.

Purpose Revealed

Twenty-two years after Joseph was sold into slavery, the day came when Joseph's teenage dream—the dream of being in a position of authority over his brothers—came true. The seven years of prosperous harvests had come and gone. Not only Egypt, but the whole region, was in the throes of a great famine. Canaan was no exception. Hearing that Egypt had food supplies for sale, Joseph's brothers traveled there. As they bowed before Joseph with their request, all the pieces came together. All the why's were answered. As Joseph revealed his identity to his brothers, assuaging their fear of retribution against them, he declared,

> ". . . I am Joseph, your brother, whom you sold into slavery in Egypt. But don't be upset and angry with yourselves for selling me to this place. It was God who sent me here ahead of you to preserve your lives. . . . He is the one who made me adviser to Pharaoh—manager of his entire palace and governor of all Egypt." (Genesis 45:4-8 NLT)

> "You intended to harm me, but *God intended it all for good.* He brought me to this position so I could save the lives of many people." (Genesis 50:20 NLT)

Decades earlier, God had promised Joseph's great-grandparents, Abraham and Sarah, that their descendants would become a great nation. God's plan for Joseph's life, a plan that saved his family from a devastating famine, was necessary for that promise to be fulfilled. The descendants of Joseph and his eleven brothers became the promised nation of Israel. And it was from this nation that our Savior, Jesus Christ, would be born. The plan for Joseph's life was a necessary detail in fulfilling God's greatest plan—salvation for all mankind.

Unexpected Good from an Unexpected Plan

After two years of my teaching the "Understanding God" class in prison, that door closed. The chaplain was presented with the opportunity to offer the inmates a theology degree they could earn through a video program certified by a Christian college. This program would build upon the spiritual foundation we had laid, so we knew this, too, was part of God's plan. By now, though, my passion for prison ministry had taken hold, and I wondered what the next step in God's plan for me would be.

A few years later, that next step was revealed when I was asked to participate in a "One Day With God Camp," a prison outreach program sponsored by Forgiven Ministries to be held at the same prison where I had taught the "Understanding God" classes. My "camp" assignment was as a volunteer mentor. I accompanied a child of an inmate to the prison where he spent the day reconnecting with his father. How moving it was to see children running into their fathers' arms, participating as a team in the relay races, and interacting as crafts were made. Just before lunch, we sang worship songs led by a prison worship team.

I was struck by how gifted this team was, particularly the worship leader. So during a break, I felt led to encourage the worship leader by telling him how blessed I was by his ministry. As we talked, I mentioned how several years earlier I had taught an "Understanding God" class at this prison. His eyes lit up. He had attended that class, and it strengthened and encouraged his faith! Although he had no release date, he no longer was filled with anger, but with the confidence that God was using him in prison to minister to inmates who needed Jesus. I was blessed to see how God's unexpected plan for my life—to teach at this prison—intersected with God's plan for this inmate's life. God was working it all for good!

Lesson Five

Surely when Joseph was in that cistern, pleading with his brothers for his life, he never thought that experience could work together *for good*. When he was sold to Potiphar as a slave and then thrown into prison—how could this work together *for good*? How could these experiences be God's *good* plan for his life? But when he stood before his brothers as the governor of Egypt, he understood how all of those harsh experiences had worked to bless him and his family.

Going through difficult or challenging times doesn't mean God's favor has left us. His favor never left Joseph, even in his darkest hours. It is often during the most trying times in our lives that we learn the most valuable lessons from God. Joseph's life is a shining example of one who didn't get discouraged even though he didn't have all of God's details; one who didn't get side-tracked even though he didn't see the end from the beginning.

Like Joseph, we need to engage in our relationship with God and draw upon his wisdom and strength. When we do what God wants us to do in the present, we will be prepared for what he has planned for our future. We need to trust God, especially when our present situation makes us wonder how God could ever work it for our good. We must trust his promise:

> And we know that all things work together *for good* to those who love God, to those who are the called according to *His* purpose. (Rom. 8:28 NKJV)

Chapter Challenge

- Engage in your relationship with God by telling him you trust his plan for your life—even if his plan includes difficult times and problematic people.

- Ask him for the patience you need in order to learn from the challenges in your present so that you are prepared for the next step in his plan.

- Be mindful of the ways God's favor is upon your life even though you can't see his purpose for the struggles you are experiencing.

- Ask God for strength to remain steadfast in your faith until he reveals the good in his plan for your life. Remember: be patient in the present as God prepares you for your future.

"Lord, even when I can't see how the struggle I am facing can *work for good*, I choose to trust you. Instead of complaining, help me to be patient and open to learn what I need to learn in this present situation, so I will be equipped to take the next step in your good plan for my life. In Jesus' name I pray. Amen."

Part II

Tough Love

Chapter 6

Embrace Adversity

He was supposed to be a help, not a hindrance. I was involved in a church ministry that was growing in breadth and influence. It was an exciting but exhausting time. As the organizational side of the ministry required more attention, the leader of this ministry felt we needed to bring on someone who could take over the detail responsibilities, freeing us up to focus more on writing and teaching. Great idea, I thought, until the person who took on this role reorganized responsibilities in a way where my voice was excluded from decisions in which I once would have been involved. I was no longer invited to meetings I had once attended. I felt marginalized and, needless to say, hurt and upset. Dare I say, even mad at this guy! Being involved in this ministry had been such a joy and blessing. I knew it was part of God's plan for me, but why did God have to bring this man into it? Adversity!

There was a part of me, that voice inside, which just wanted to throw in the towel and walk away. But God's Spirit voice countered: "Practice what you teach." I had often taught students the Biblical pattern that Jesus gave us for dealing with conflict and disagreement among believers. Jesus taught that if we are offended, we are to go to that person and try to resolve the issue one-on-one. But who wants to do that?

It's not easy to go to the person who has offended you. It's much easier, it's even our natural inclination, to go to others and complain about how badly this person has treated us, right? I had a choice in facing this adversity. Listen to my voice or God's voice? Continue to complain about how badly I was being treated or talk to this man and try to resolve the issue?

It wasn't easy. It wasn't comfortable. But I did it. I shared with him how I felt, and then he shared with me the reasoning behind his decision. He said his intention wasn't to hurt me, but rather to streamline the organization. So, he would not undo what he had done. It wasn't the answer I wanted or expected to hear. It wasn't an answer I agreed with. I thought that by speaking with him personally he would change his mind and my role of influence would be restored. It was not, and our conversation closed with a cordial goodbye. But now I had another choice. Would I forgive him for the hurt his decision had caused? Could I accept that fact that I wasn't going to change his mind? Would I still be faithful to God's plan for me and continue to serve in this ministry, or would I leave?

As I prayed about this situation, God spoke to my heart to forgive this man for the hurt he caused and to trust God—trust he would somehow, someway, work it for my good. Even though it wasn't what I *felt* like doing, I made the difficult choice to forgive, and God healed the hurt. In time, this man was asked to be part of another ministry and moved on. But God used this man and this experience to teach me an important and necessary lesson about facing adversity: listen to God's voice instead of the voice of my feelings. It was a lesson that underscores how God uses adversity to chasten us, and how he intends this chastening to be for our good.

Certainly it is not hard for us to see the good in God's love and mercy, in his grace and forgiveness, in his care and compassion for us. But chastening? When God uses adversity to chasten us, it is hard to see the good because it feels so bad. But look at what we read in Hebrews 12:6: ". . . the Lord disciplines the one he loves, and he *chastens* everyone he accepts as his son." A bittersweet scripture! We rejoice that we are the children of God whom he loves, but not so thrilled that as his children, we will be chastened. Yet chastening is an important part of becoming mature disciples of Christ.

Typically, when we hear the word "chasten," we think of punishment. And certainly, there is a chastening to correct disobedience. The story of Jonah is an example. He experienced the ordeal of being in the belly of a great fish because God needed to correct his disobedient behavior. We'll learn more about this corrective chastening in the next chapter. But for now, let's turn our focus to another definition of chastening—one that Joseph would have understood.

Training

The word "chastening" used in Hebrews 12 comes from the Greek words *paideuo* or *paideia* which have a two-fold meaning.[1] They refer to discipline that corrects errant behavior, but they also refer to the discipline of training—instruction that molds or perfects one's character. So when the Lord chastens us, he may be training us with a discipline that may push us to our limits, not because he is punishing us, or is displeased with us, but rather because he is molding and perfecting us. God can use adversity to foster endurance necessary for spiritual maturity.

We all face adversity in our lives. We may not face the same adversity in the same way, but we will face adversity of some kind. For me it was while I was involved in a church ministry. For you it may be a financial need or a health issue. It can be in the form of loss—a broken relationship, a betrayal, the death of a loved one, sudden unemployment. And we don't just experience one adversity in life and then we're done. The list goes on, as does the degree and frequency of adversity in our lives. It has been said that you're either coming out of a trial, in the middle of a trial, or headed into one. No matter the type of trial or adversity we may experience, what is important is how we respond to it—to know what to do and what not to do. So let's return to that first generation of Israelites who

---

[1] https://bible.knowing-jesus.com/strongs/G3811

experienced the miraculous deliverance from Egyptian slavery—who saw the waters of the Red Sea part and walked safely to the other side as they journeyed through the wilderness to the Promised Land. And let's learn what not to do!

What Not to Do

After traveling through the wilderness, the Israelites finally arrived at the border of the Promised Land. From their camp they could see the vast land which lay before them. This was the land God promised to their honored patriarchs, Abraham, Isaac, and Jacob. They were on the precipice of one of the most significant moments in their history. What lay before them was the privilege of being *the* generation through whom God's promise would be fulfilled—a promise Abraham knew would not be realized in his lifetime but would one day by his descendants. And they were that chosen generation!

Before entering this Promised Land, however, God instructed Moses to send twelve men to spy out and explore the land for forty days. The people waited in great anticipation. As the twelve spies returned to camp, the people could see them carrying great clusters of grapes so large they had to be carried on poles by two men. They also saw an abundance of figs and pomegranates. Imagine the excitement! These Israelites had been eating manna day after day for months. It was nourishment, but certainly it had become monotonous. Now they saw luscious grapes, pomegranates, and figs. What joy filled the camp!

The twelve spies stood before the people to give their formal report. Everyone became silent, eager to hear every word. Ten of the spies declared, "It is a bountiful country—a land flowing with milk and honey. Look at its fruit!" Cheers and shouts of joy broke out. Then they continued their report with an unexpected "but." "*But* the people living there are powerful and their towns are large and fortified. We even saw giants there." [2]

---

[2] Numbers 13:27-28 NLT

This negative report turned the rejoicing to panic. Quickly, the two remaining spies, Joshua and Caleb, stood up before the people, rebutting the report and declaring, "Let's go at once and take the land. We can certainly conquer it!" But all through the night, the ten spies continued to spread their negative report. And the people *embraced* it. As the negative report gained momentum, the people began to weep and wail. Their voices rose in protest, "Why did the Lord take us to this country only to have us die in battle? ... Wouldn't it be better if we went back to Egypt?"[3] They even plotted to choose a new leader to take them there.

Because the people *embraced the negative report*, their hearts were filled with fear, and they responded with despairing cries and faithless complaints. Instead, they should have fortified their faith in God by reminding themselves once again of the many times in the past he had brought deliverance and provision. They should have turned to God with prayers of praise, expressing their confidence in him:

> *Lord, when we were pursued by the Egyptians, you parted the Red Sea!*
> *When we ran out of water, you provided water from the Rock!*
> *When we needed food, you provided the manna and quail!*
> *It doesn't matter if the cities are fortified.*
> *It doesn't matter if there are giants in the land.*
> *We know you will give us victory as we occupy this Promised Land.*

But no such words of praise were heard. The Israelites embraced the negative report instead of embracing the One who had always proven to be their deliverer. They allowed the adversity to consume them with fear and doubt. As a result, this generation never possessed the promise. They died in the wilderness. Instead it would be their children, the next generation, who would fulfill God's promise to Abraham. Their children would be the ones who would leave the legacy as *the* generation who possessed the Promised Land.

If we are honest, how often do we find ourselves reacting the same way when facing adversity—complaining about the discomfort

---

[3] Numbers 13:30; 14:1-4 NLT

instead of praising God for what we believe he can do? So we must choose wisely what voices we listen to, what messages we embrace, because today there are more than "ten voices" broadcasting negativity. No matter where we turn, we hear negative voices in what we read, watch, and hear. Yet in the midst of all this negativity, we must remember the positive voice—the voice of God's Word that contains his promises and documents his faithfulness to us.[4]

Perhaps it was the unexpectedness of what the spies encountered in the Promised Land that crippled their faith and compelled them to give a negative report. Since this was the land God had chosen for them, they may have expected that it would be a land easily possessed, not filled with giants. Often it is the same with us. When we face adversity, its unexpectedness can blindside us, inclining us to tune into voices of doubt and fear, especially when we are doing what God wants us to do. Fortunately, we can look to the apostle Paul who taught by example how to respond to adversity when it arrives unexpectedly at your door. Or in Paul's case, at a prison cell door!

What to Do

Before Paul was known as an apostle, he was known as Saul the Persecutor. Deeply concerned about the growing number of Christ-followers after the resurrection of Jesus, Paul made it his mission to stamp out what he perceived as a heretical movement. His persecution of Jesus-followers began in Jerusalem, but his desire was to take this persecution to regions beyond this holy city. Yet on the way to Damascus, with a court order allowing him great latitude to arrest and execute Christians, God interrupted Paul's plan. In an unexpected place, to an unexpected man, Jesus appeared to Paul. His conversion was dramatic and instantaneous. The one who had been a leading persecutor of Christians was now passionately leading others to Christ.

God's plan for Paul would be to share the gospel, the good news

---

[4] Examples of specific scriptures of God's promises to us can be found in Chapter 10, *Embrace His Sword.*

of salvation, to unexpected people—the Gentiles. Paul had been schooled in Jewish theology that regarded Gentiles as "unclean." He prided himself on keeping the Levitical laws of the Jewish religion, so he would never have eaten with a Gentile, never have even entered the home of a Gentile. But now God was calling him to preach the gospel of salvation *to* the Gentiles! Paul embraced this plan, a decision many in his day would have considered wildly unexpected. Paul the Persecutor became Paul the Preacher—a missionary to the Gentiles.

His first missionary trip was to Galatia and Cyprus, where he and his partner, Barnabas, preached the gospel, performed miracles, and established churches. By 49 A.D. Paul was ready to embark on his second missionary trip, this time with Silas. They traveled to Phrygia and Galatia with a plan to preach in the province of Asia. But the Holy Spirit prevented them from going in that direction, so they decided to go north to Bithynia. Again, the Holy Spirit intervened and changed their travel plans. During the night, God gave Paul a vision instructing him to travel and minister in Macedonia.

Being obedient to God, Paul and Silas left for Philippi, a major city in Macedonia. Learning that there were Philippians who gathered by a river to pray, Paul and Silas joined them and shared the gospel of Jesus. Many believed and were baptized. Day after day, the two met with people at the riverbank. Even more people believed and were baptized. Seeing the response of the Philippians, Paul and Silas were confident they were centered in God's will.

Each day as they traveled to the riverbank, however, there was a demon-possessed psychic, a slave girl, who harangued them.[5] Finally, in exasperation, Paul turned to her and cast out the demon. The slave girl was immediately healed. How this mighty miracle thrilled the hearts of those who witnessed God's power to deliver the girl. But not everyone was thrilled. When the young woman's masters realized her ability to make money for them was gone, they were furious. They dragged Paul and Silas to the city officials, where they were stripped and beaten with wooden rods. From there they were thrown

---

[5] Acts 16:16-24

73

into a maximum-security jail. Their legs were clamped in irons. An unexpected turn of events! Everything had been going great. People believed in Jesus, an awesome miracle had taken place, yet now Paul and Silas found themselves beaten and chained in a dungeon, facing possible execution. Adversity!

If this happened to you, how would you react? After all, God directed you with a powerful vision to go to Macedonia. You were being obedient, doing exactly what God wanted you to do, yet here you are now, chained in prison, your body racked with pain, not knowing what the morning will bring. Paul and Silas find themselves in a similar situation to their ancestor, Joseph. Unjustly imprisoned, doing the right things, but ending up in unexpected, uncomfortable places. We know what Joseph did. What did Paul and Silas do?

As they sat chained in a prison cell, Paul and Silas began to pray and sing hymns of *praise* to God. They didn't complain, whine, or bemoan their condition. Their feelings did not govern their actions. Instead they sang praises to God. I can imagine Paul's song of prayer and praise:[6]

Lord, when I was stoned almost to the point of death, you healed me.
When I was beaten, you restored my strength.
When I was pursued, you made a way of escape.
When I was shipwrecked, you spared me.
When I was in need, you provided. You are worthy to be praised.

Paul and Silas faced this unexpected adversity in an unexpected way —with prayer and songs of praise, declaring their confidence in the Lord. Their response was so unexpected that it made a powerful impression on the other prisoners who were listening.

At midnight, God sent an earthquake which broke open the jail doors and loosened their chains, but not one of the prisoners chose to escape. Instead, they all remained with Paul and Silas, amazed by the power of God. Even the jailer and his family became believers!

---

[6] 2 Corinthians 11:24-26

Paul and Silas were powerful witnesses for Christ because of their choice to praise God in the midst of their adversity.

Without the unexpected detour to Macedonia and the resulting imprisonment, there would have been no need for God's power to be revealed in an earthquake that opened prison doors and, ultimately, brought the jailer and his family to salvation. Although in the moment adversity can be painful, uncomfortable and inconvenient, it can also be part of God's plan that accomplishes a greater purpose. It did for Paul and Silas. It did for Joseph and his family. And it does for us today.

Lesson Six

How sad that the legacy of the wilderness generation of Israelites would be their failure to embrace faith in the power of God when they encountered unexpected adversity. God intended the adversity to develop and foster great faith. But they let their feelings drive their behavior. So when the unexpected happened, they hurled complaints against God instead of drawing close to him in faith and with praise.

As we read the story of these Israelites, we shake our heads in disbelief. But at the same time, it is not difficult to see ourselves in them—especially when we experience the discomfort of unexpected adversity. When we are doing everything right, when we are being obedient to God, and everything is going wrong, we, too, tend to whine and complain. All too often, like the Israelites, our instinct is to embrace the negative report, to believe the worst, to be consumed with fear and anxiety. But it's in these moments that we can choose to follow the example of Paul and Silas. Instead of complaining and embracing the negative, we can pray for deliverance. And, while we are waiting in that prison of adversity, we can praise God for who he is and what he has already done for us.

Certainly, while we are experiencing adversity, we may not *feel* like praising God, but as disciples of Christ we are not to be governed by our feelings. Instead, we are to praise God for all his marvelous works of grace and love. Praise in the face of adversity is an expression of our confidence and trust in God to *work all things for our good*[7]—a hallmark of spiritual maturity.

Chapter Challenge

- If you are experiencing adversity in your life, the negativity that comes with discomfort and pain can overwhelm you. Anxiety can consume you. Instead of bemoaning the situation, do what is counterintuitive—sing a song to the Lord for the good things he *has done* in your life. Sing about a time he has healed you or healed someone you love, the time he has met a financial need or protected a loved one.

- If you are not a singer, then journal your praise or share a testimony of his faithfulness with a friend or relative.

- Whether you sing it, write it, or speak it, fill your heart with praise to our God, because praise tunes out the negative voice that breeds discouragement and defeat. Praise expresses your confidence in his faithful plan for your life.

- Trust God. Trust his plan for your life.

---

[7] Acts 16:25; Romans 8:28 NKJV

Chapter 7

Embrace His Chastening

I knew better. I should have declined, but how could I resist the emphatic plea of my grandson: Would I *please* play a video game with him—Super Mario Brothers? I was reasonably competent with several Wii video games and suggested we play one of those. But he, undaunted by my protest, proceeded to give me a 15-second tutorial, assuring me I would catch on quickly. I did not!

Within seconds, my Mario fell off the grid and died. So, we started over again. Finally, after a few false starts, I got the hang of it. As my Mario raced along, I suddenly found myself ahead of my grandson's Mario. Then came the outburst. Inexplicably, I had caused his Mario to die. I'm not sure how, but apparently I was supposed to save him with a Yoshi. Unsure of even what a Yoshi was, I now faced a grandson in meltdown mode with cries of blame being hurled at me. Immediately, his mother stepped in to discipline: "Stop crying and blaming your grandmother! If you don't stop, I'll turn off the game."

With tears flowing down his face, he didn't let up. "But she didn't get my Yoshi! My Mario died because she didn't wait for me!" As his tirade continued, she walked over to the Wii and turned it off. Stunned at what she had done, he pleaded with her to resume the game. "But Mom, you only gave me one warning! You only told me once. Even God gave Jonah two chances!" Her response: "Well, honey, I'm not God, and the Wii stays off."

In the moment, my grandson viewed my daughter's decision to turn off the Wii as being unfair, even mean. He could not comprehend how her decision was an act of love. She could have ignored his behavior, but because she loved him, she made the effort to correct what was unacceptable. And because God loves us, we too experience his chastening—chastening that may not be pleasant in the moment, but is meant to correct our errant behavior.

In the last chapter, we explored the meaning of chastening as it pertains to adversity that fosters spiritual maturity. But in this chapter, we will explore the flipside meaning of chastening: corrective discipline. We'll look a little closer at the man my grandson used as his defense—the man whose disobedience evoked God's corrective chastening but also whose God gave him a second chance: Jonah.

Chastening a Prophet

Jonah was a prophet of God from the region of Galilee during the eighth century, B.C. In this ancient world, prophets were spiritual leaders used as links between God and his people. Jonah had been faithful to relay God's prophetic word to the king of Israel, but when God instructed Jonah to go to Nineveh with a message of judgment, Jonah refused. Instead of heading toward Nineveh, Jonah went in the opposite direction.

The Bible doesn't provide a clear reason for Jonah's unwillingness. Nineveh was a great Assyrian city, and the Assyrians were historically the enemies and oppressors of Israel. Perhaps he feared an Israelite prophet delivering a warning of impending destruction would not be welcomed with open arms. A more likely reason, however, was a greater fear that the Ninevites would repent, and God would relent. As an Israelite, Jonah undoubtedly believed the destruction of Nineveh was well-deserved.

So Jonah fled to Joppa and boarded a ship on its way to Tarshish, attempting to get as far away from God as possible. Jonah was 180 degrees from where God wanted him to be, deep inside the hold of this ship, falsely secure in the belief that he had successfully hidden himself from God. He was so confident that he fell peacefully asleep on a cot below deck.

It is confounding that a prophet of God would think he could run and hide from the Lord. Yet Jonah exemplifies how faulty our reasoning can become when we choose to disobey God. Jonah deluded himself into thinking that by changing his location, he could hide from God. But God knew exactly where Jonah was, and sent a great wind to cause a violent storm that threatened to capsize the ship. This storm was sent because of Jonah's disobedience.

As the tempest intensified, the crew threw cargo overboard to lighten the ship. They even prayed to their gods but to no avail. They panicked as Jonah slept. Finally, the captain went below deck and awakened Jonah, imploring him to cry out to his god. Jonah accompanied the captain deck side, but there is no account of Jonah praying. Certainly you don't want to pray to God when you are trying to hide from him.

The storm continued to rage. By now the ship's crew perceived it was no ordinary storm. To determine who was the cause of this tempest, they cast lots—much like what we would call drawing straws. Jonah drew the short straw and confessed he was running from his God. When the crew heard his story, they questioned him: "Why did you do this? How do we stop the storm?" [1] Jonah's solution was for the crew to throw him overboard. The sailors were reluctant to cast him into the sea, so with renewed effort they tried to row to shore. But the storm only became fiercer. At last, the sailors picked Jonah up and threw him into the sea. Immediately the storm ceased. Recognizing the power of Jonah's God, they abandoned their gods and worshiped the Lord. While the ship's crew was worshiping God, Jonah sank into the depths, seaweed wrapped around his neck. With his lungs bursting, certain of imminent death, Jonah suddenly became aware of a great fish looming nearby. An overwhelming fear gripped him as the fish swam closer and opened its mouth. The fear of drowning was replaced by the terror of being digested! As Jonah was being swallowed, he never would have imagined that this great fish would be the way of his salvation from a watery grave.

---

[1] Jonah 1:10-16

In the belly of that fish, the smells were horrific, the slime nauseous, the darkness chilling. Hours passed and turned into days. Finally, after three days, Jonah did what he had failed to do while on the ship: he turned his thoughts to the Lord. He repented of his disobedience. He would go to Nineveh. Jonah also promised to offer sacrifices of praise to God for his deliverance. When the Lord heard Jonah's repentant prayer, he "ordered the fish to spit Jonah out onto the beach."[2] The mercy that Jonah feared God would extend to the Ninevites if they repented was the same mercy that Jonah gratefully accepted. God gave him a second chance to be obedient.

> Then the Lord spoke to Jonah *a second time*: "Get up and go to the great city of Nineveh, and deliver the message I have given you." *This time* Jonah obeyed the Lord's command. (Jonah 3:1-3 NLT)

The Ninevites

Jonah traveled to Nineveh, a major city so large it would take three days to walk through it. Upon his arrival, he shouted to the crowds in the streets the message God had given him: "Forty days from now Nineveh will be destroyed."[3] The Ninevites who heard Jonah's message believed that his God had the power to do what Jonah declared. The message spread like wildfire. People dressed in burlap, an action expressing genuine remorse; the king even sent out a decree declaring a city-wide fast. He exhorted everyone to earnestly pray to Jonah's God, and to turn from their evil and violent ways. And God saw their genuine repentance.

> When God saw what they did and how they turned from their evil ways, he relented and did not bring on them destruction he had threatened. (Jonah 3:10)

Because our God is a God of mercy, he responds to genuine repentance with kindness. He withdrew his plan of destruction and gave the Ninevites a second chance.

---

[2] Jonah 2:9-10 NLT
[3] Jonah 3:1-10 NLT

Lesson Seven

There are some who read the Old Testament and only see a God of judgment. They fail to see how his mercy trumps every judgment, how he administers corrective chastening out of love. God didn't send the storm to be cruel. He didn't send the fish and allow Jonah to sit in that dark and ominous place to be mean. He sent the storm and gave Jonah a fish experience because God wanted to get Jonah's attention and give him the *opportunity* to repent—to correct his disobedient behavior. The storm and the fish were what God used to give Jonah a second chance. And Jonah's second chance was what God used to give the Ninevites their second chance.

As we follow Christ, because we are in the process of becoming like him, there will be times when God uses a storm or even something like Jonah's fish experience to get our attention. He wants to reveal to us disobedience in our lives, to expose attitudes or behaviors that need to be changed. Corrective chastening is not pleasant in the moment, but when it brings about a change in heart—a repentant heart—it becomes a blessing.

Chapter Challenge

- Are you experiencing a time of corrective chastening? Is God trying to bring your attention to an area of disobedience in your life? Or is he making you aware of an attitude or behavior that needs to be changed? If so, do what Jonah ultimately did. Do what the Ninevites did. Repent. Acknowledge your shortcoming and ask for forgiveness. But don't just say you're sorry. Remember repentance goes beyond regret or remorse for what we have said or done. Repentance requires change!

- Embrace his forgiveness and make the choice to change. Watch how God responds to genuine repentance with mercy—giving you a second chance.

Because repentance is so vital to our relationship with God, we need to delve a little deeper into the necessity of *genuine* repentance, which we will do in the next chapter.

Chapter 8

Embrace Repentance

My fascination with all things Titanic never wanes. It's the "what if" stories I find most intriguing, especially the one about the binoculars. Yes, binoculars! A few hectic days before the maiden voyage of the Titanic, Second Officer David Blair was transferred to another ship and replaced by Chief Officer Henry Wilde, who had more experience than Blair. In the haste of this last-minute change, it is believed that Blair failed to hand off the key to the storage locker which held the ship's binoculars. As a result, the lookout crew had to rely on their eyesight to spot hazards. Fred Fleet, a sailor on lookout duty who first spotted the iceberg, testified that by the time they were able to see it with their naked eyes, it was too late to turn the massive ocean liner out of harm's way.[1]

What if the crew had had the key to that storage locker? *What if* they had located binoculars elsewhere in the ship? Could the collision with the iceberg have been avoided? This is but one *what if* that could have altered a tragic moment in history. Yet there is a *what if* that could have affected all of humanity. This *what if* takes us back to the beginning with Adam and Eve. It's the tragic moment when they ate fruit from the forbidden tree—the Tree of Knowledge of Good and Evil. *What if* they hadn't eaten it?

---

[1] Tibbets, Graham, (2007, Aug. 29) Key that could have saved the Titanic. *The Telegraph*. Retrieved from https://www.telegraph.co.uk

Eating that fruit was an act of blatant disobedience. God had clearly warned them not to eat the fruit of this tree or they would die. Although they weren't immediately struck dead when they ate the fruit, they did experience a spiritual death. And, tragically, because of their disobedience sin entered humanity, altering man's nature. No longer would mankind possess a sinless nature; it was replaced with a sin-broken nature. So, when God—who is holy—entered the garden, how they must have trembled with fear as his voice called out to them: "Where are you? Why are you hiding? . . . Did you eat from the tree I told you not to eat from?"[2]

Adam's response? "It was the woman you gave me who gave me the fruit, and I ate it." In other words Adam is saying, "God, it's your fault for giving me Eve, and it's Eve's fault because she gave me the fruit." He justified his disobedience by shifting the blame. Eve's response? "The serpent deceived me . . . That's why I ate it." Eve pointed the finger at Satan, the serpent, as her justification for disobedience.[3]

But *what if* their responses to God's questions had been different? Instead of the justifications, blame-shifting, and excuses, what if they had responded with genuine repentance? What if they had confessed their disobedience? We will never know the answer to these questions, but we do know how God responded when Jonah and the Ninevites repented. We can also see the necessity of genuine repentance by looking at the actions of two great kings who, like Adam and Eve, were disobedient, but responded in two different ways. One like Adam and Eve and the other with a heart of repentance.

An Unrepentant Heart

King Saul was anointed as the first king of Israel. He was tall in stature and had the look of a king, but lacked the confidence to match. After being anointed by God, the Spirit of the Lord came

---

[2] Genesis 3:9, 11
[3] Genesis 3:12-13 NLT

upon Saul in a powerful way, and he was changed "into a different person."[4] He possessed a confidence he had never had before. At the beginning of King Saul's reign, he was obedient, keeping God's commandments. When he went into battle against the Philistines, God was with him, and he was victorious. But with success, King Saul's attitude toward God changed. He was more interested in doing things his way instead of God's way. He developed a habit of bending the rules and obeying God halfway, offering justifications and excuses. Such was the case when God instructed King Saul to lead his army in God's judgment against the Amalekites.

God's instructions were straightforward: destroy all the Amalekites and their livestock. King Saul and his army did defeat the Amalekites, but they spared the king and the best of the livestock. They spared "everything, in fact, that appealed to them. They destroyed only what was worthless or of poor quality."[5] In response, God sent the prophet Samuel to confront King Saul. When Samuel arrived, Saul happily declared how he had obeyed God's instructions. Samuel countered sharply, "Then what is all the bleating of sheep and goats and the lowing of cattle I hear?" Without missing a beat, Saul admitted,

> "It's true that the army spared the best of the sheep, goats, and cattle ... But they (the men) are going to sacrifice them to the Lord your God. We have destroyed everything else."
> (1 Samuel 15:15 NLT)

He justified his disobedience by disguising his greed with the intention to use the animals as a sacrifice to God. Samuel rebutted Saul—this wasn't the kind of sacrifice God desired. And then he asked,

> "Why haven't you obeyed the Lord? Why did you rush for the plunder and do what was evil in the Lord's sight?"
> (1 Samuel 15:19 NLT)

---

[4] 1 Samuel 10:6
[5] 1 Samuel 15:9,14NLT

But Saul continued to deny he had done anything wrong. His heart was unrepentant. Samuel then relayed to him God's judgment for his disobedience: "Because you have rejected the command of the Lord, he has rejected you as king."[6] That got Saul's attention! Finally, he admitted his disobedience. Yet incredulously, even in his confession, Saul still blamed others:

> "Yes, I have sinned. I have disobeyed your instructions and
> the Lord's command, for I was afraid of the people and did
> what they demanded." (1 Samuel 15:24 NLT)

King Saul never genuinely repented. The reason for his lack of repentance can be traced back to what he did immediately after defeating the Amalekites. It was an action that revealed what was truly in his heart. "Saul went to the town of Carmel to set up a monument to himself."[7] King Saul was not interested in glorifying God for the victory, but rather in glorifying himself. He was more interested in currying the favor of the people than in doing what was pleasing to God. And because of Saul's unrepentant heart, God rejected him as king.

A Man After God's Own Heart

In Saul's place, God chose a man named David and anointed him to be king while he was still a young shepherd boy. His journey to kingship, however, was not an easy one; it was long and arduous, filled with intrigue and danger. David was pursued by a jealous King Saul, but it was during these fugitive years that he learned to draw close to God for wisdom, guidance, and strength.

God chose David to be king because he was a "man after God's own heart."[8] His devotion to God is apparent when we read his poetic words of prayer and praise penned in the book of Psalms. David wrote:

---

[6] 1 Samuel 15:23 NLT
[7] 1 Samuel 15:12 NLT
[8] Acts 13:14

> "One thing I ask from the Lord, this only do I seek: that I may dwell in the house of the Lord all the days of my life, to gaze on the beauty of the Lord and to seek him in his temple." (Psalm 27:4)

David was the king of Israel for forty years, and God blessed his reign tremendously. God gave him victory over his enemies, expanded his kingdom, and entered into a special covenant with David. During the second half of his reign, however, he committed a grievous sin. He committed adultery with Bathsheba, the wife of Uriah, one of David's army commanders. When David learned Bathsheba was pregnant, he tried to cover up his sin of adultery by sending her husband to certain death at the battle front. His plan was to deceive people into believing that she was pregnant by her husband, not by David. He tried to hide his sin, but, just as Jonah learned, no sin is hidden from God. So, God sent the prophet Nathan to confront David:

> "Why, then, have you despised the word of the Lord and done this horrible deed? For you have murdered Uriah the Hittite with the sword of the Ammonites and stolen his wife." (2 Samuel 12:9-10 NLT)

How did David respond? Without excuses, justifications, or blame-shifting, his confession was heartfelt and sincere. "I have sinned against the Lord."[9] Certainly, David suffered consequences for his sins of adultery and murder. He suffered the death of his child, and because of his actions, murder and violence plagued his family. His grown son, Absalom, whom David dearly loved, would lead an unsuccessful revolt against David. But God did not abandon him in those consequences. Mercifully, he did not reject David as king as he had Saul. Nor did God revoke his promise that through David's lineage an eternal king would come—our Savior Jesus Christ.

---

[9] 2 Samuel 12:13 NLT

A Repentant Heart

When you compare the sins of David, though, with those of Saul's, something seems amiss. David committed adultery and murder, while Saul merely failed to kill the Amalekite king and all of the livestock. It seems David should have received a much harsher judgment than Saul. And if David wasn't rejected as king, then it only seems fair that Saul shouldn't have been rejected either. It doesn't make sense until you understand that God looks at the heart.

Where did Saul go after defeating the Amalekites? To Carmel to erect a monument to himself. What did he do when confronted with his sin? He responded with justifications and excuses. When God looked at Saul's heart, he saw the heart of a man who sought to glorify himself instead of glorifying God. He saw a heart of rebellion.

Now look at the evidence of what was in David's heart. When he was victorious on the battlefield, he didn't seek glory for himself, he gave glory to God. He lifted up his voice with songs of praise, extolling God for all of *his* mighty power. And when David sinned, he responded with a contrite and repentant heart.

> "Have mercy on me, O God, because of your unfailing love. Because of your great compassion, blot out the stain of my sins. Wash me clean from my guilt. Purify me from my sin … Against you, and you alone, have I sinned; I have done what is evil in your sight … Create in me a clean heart, O God. Renew a loyal spirit within me. Do not banish me from your presence, and don't take your Holy Spirit from me." (Psalm 51:1-2, 4, 10-11 NLT)

David was far from perfect, but he possessed an unparalleled heart of love for God, expressed in worship. And when he failed God, he expressed his love with genuine repentance. That is why David is called a "man after God's own heart."

Lesson Eight

Being a disciple of Christ means being a student of God's Word. Not just learning about the characters and events in the Bible, but applying the lessons to real life. The lesson from Saul is that when the Holy Spirit convicts you of sin, don't make excuses or justifications. Don't try to shift blame onto others.

The lesson from David is that no matter how great a sin you commit, how terribly short of God's glorious standard you fall, turn to God with a genuine heart of repentance. We can take solace in these great truths that David understood about our God: "You (Lord) will not reject a broken and repentant heart …"[10] And as David wrote in that same psalm, when we embrace repentance, God removes the stain of sin and creates in us a clean heart!

Chapter Challenge

- Take a moment to honestly examine your heart once again. Is there *any* sin in your life you have been condoning? Perhaps you even have some logical-sounding justifications. Nevertheless, down deep, you know it is sin. God hasn't sent a prophet to confront you like he did with David or violent storm and a great fish as he did with Jonah, but he has allowed his Holy Spirit to convict you and make you uncomfortable.

- Confess the sin now—name it without justifications or excuses. Be honest and sincere, ask for forgiveness, and know that our God will not reject your broken and repentant heart. He will remove the stain of sin and give you a clean heart!

---

[10] Psalm 51:17 NLT

Part III

Transforming Power

Chapter 9

Embrace Thankfulness

It was a perfect night: cool enough to sit around a bonfire, but warm enough to sit without coats or gloves. The babies were fast asleep in the lakeside cottage. Now the adults could relax, enjoying the fire and the reflection of the moon on the water. As we engaged in lively conversation, our eyes drew upward. The Michigan sky was a grand display of brilliant stars, shooting and racing across the sky. We were filled with wonder and awe at God's power to speak these heavenly bodies into being.

I think David must have experienced a night like this. He, too, must have felt the insignificance of humanity as he pondered the breathtaking handiwork of God, the star-Maker and planet-Creator, for he wrote:

> I look up at your macro-skies, dark and enormous, your handmade sky-jewelry, moon and stars are mounted in their settings. Then I look at my micro-self and wonder, Why do you bother with us? Why take a second look our way? (Psalm 8:3-4 MSG)

When we reflect on how blessed we are—that this macro-God not only bothers, but even cares about the micro-us—we can identify with yet another question David posed: "What can I offer the Lord for all that he has done for me?"[1] In other words, David was saying, "What can mere mortals offer this star-Maker, salvation-Giver, blessing Provider?" With great insight, David provided an answer:

> I will lift up the cup of salvation and *praise the Lord's name* for saving me. . . I will offer you a *sacrifice of thanksgiving* and call upon the name of the Lord. (Psalm 116:13, 17 NLT)

What can we offer the Lord for all he has done for us? Praise *and* thanksgiving. We can praise the Lord for who he is, but also thank him for all he has done. The Psalms are full of David's words of praise offered unto God, but he did not forget to also offer jubilant words of thanksgiving as well. He even exhorts us to

> . . . *give thanks* for the Lord for his unfailing love and his wonderful deeds for mankind. . . . sacrifice *thank offerings* and tell of his works with songs of joy. (Psalm 107:21-22)

In the days of King David, the people fully understood what the sacrifice of thanksgiving, known as a "thank offering," involved. They knew exactly what this sacrifice entailed—what animal to bring and how to present it. A "thank offering," however, wasn't a mandated sacrifice to be brought to the Lord on a certain day in a certain month. It was a voluntary sacrifice, offered to God whenever they desired to express thankfulness to him.

Fortunately, the thank offering the Lord desires from us is no longer an animal sacrifice. Instead it is a sacrifice of thanksgiving expressed with heartfelt words of gratefulness for all that he has done for us. The apostle Paul gives us this instruction:

> Sing and make music *from your heart* to the Lord, always giving thanks to God the Father for *everything*, in the name of our Lord Jesus Christ. (Ephesians 5:19-20)

We are to give thanks for everything! But there is more. God wants us to express our gratitude not only after he answers our prayers, but

---

[1] Psalm 116:12 NLT

also as we ask, even while we await his answer.

> Do not be anxious about anything, but in every situation, by prayer and petition, *with thanksgiving*, present your requests to God. (Philippians 4:6)

When we bring our prayerful requests to God—for our family, our friends, our church, our nation—we are to ask *with thanksgiving*. Perhaps this is why David instructed us to "offer a sacrifice of thanksgiving *and* call on the name of the Lord." The *thanking* and the *asking* go hand-in-hand. Yet how much more asking do we do than thanking?

As I contemplated these Scriptures, I was challenged to examine how I was praying. And to be honest, more often than not, my asking far outweighed my thanking. Yes, I was grateful for God's blessings in my life, but those expressions of thankfulness tended toward generalities instead of specific words of gratitude. I would praise him for being a *good* God but failed to thank him for the specific and abundant ways in which he has been *good* to me.

I realized my prayers needed to be filled with a greater measure of thankfulness, because thankfulness is an offering that touches God's heart. And, it disappoints him when we fail to offer it—a lesson we learn from Christ's encounter with ten lepers.

Ten Lepers

The journey to the cross lay before Jesus as he pressed on to Jerusalem for the last time. On his way, he and his disciples decided to spend the night in a small village along the border between Samaria and Galilee. As he approached the village, just on its outskirts Jesus heard a ragtag huddle of men crying out, "Jesus, Master, have mercy on us!"[2] With all their strength they shouted their desperate plea. They shouted because they were outcasts, lepers deemed unclean.

---

[2] Luke 17:13 NLT

Lepers were required to live outside their cities in what were known as leper colonies. They were not to touch or even get close to anyone healthy: the disease was contagious. Lepers could not live with their families. They lost their livelihoods, were reduced to begging, and were restricted from worshiping in the temple or entering the synagogues. They became social outcasts who lived a rejected, desolate life. Yet their misery went beyond this social rejection and isolation.

Lepers would watch helplessly as the voracious bacteria created lesions and white patches of oozing sores on their skin, destroyed skin tissue, and left behind deformed fingers, toes, eyes, ears, and noses, giving them an unearthly appearance. Nerve endings were destroyed, which resulted in the inability to feel pain, causing further disfiguration as lepers unknowingly injured themselves.

The Bible doesn't state to what extent this disease had ravaged the bodies of these ten men. But there is little doubt that beyond the physical pain of leprosy, these men had suffered severely from the emotional trauma and stigma of the disease. But now they had a glimmer of hope. They had heard about a man named Jesus who performed miracles for the deaf, the blind, and the lame. If he could do that, he certainly could heal them. But since they couldn't go near him—or anyone—they had to get his attention before he disappeared through the village gates, taking with him their only hope. So they shouted. They cried out.

Imagine the desperation in their anguished plea, willing with every ounce of their being that Jesus would hear them and respond with mercy. And he did! Jesus instructed them, "Go, show yourselves to the priests."[3] This may seem like a strange response to us, but those lepers knew exactly what those words meant. They would be healed. Having been schooled in the law of Moses, they knew a person who had been deemed unclean due to a skin disease must be examined by a priest to be declared clean. And once a person was declared clean, he was no longer an outcast. He would be welcomed back into his family and embraced by his community. He could once

---

[3] Luke 17:14; Leviticus 14:1-9

again worship in the temple and be taught in the synagogue. So all ten men obeyed Jesus' instruction and immediately turned toward the village.

As they made their way to be examined by the priests, they were healed. Envision their joy, their relief, their absolute wonderment as their lesions and deformities disappeared! With elation they realized they no longer were required to shout, "I'm a leper. I'm unclean." Like a team of baseball players winning the World Series, the ten men must have jumped up and down in jubilation, "high fives" all around. These men who had been living a death sentence would now be able to return to a life with the living. All that was left to do was go to the priests and be declared clean.

Yet there were only nine men standing before the temple priests. One had turned back. There was something he wanted to do *first*. Before being declared clean, before reuniting with his family and friends, this leper wanted to express his genuine thankfulness to Jesus.

> One of them, when he saw he was healed, came back, praising God in a loud voice. He threw himself at Jesus' feet and thanked him. (Luke 17:15-16)

This healed leper didn't shake Jesus' hand or offer a demure thank-you. His was an exuberant offering of thankfulness expressed with words of praise and actions of gratefulness. He not only thanked and praised God with a loud voice over and over again, but he lay prostrate at Jesus' feet as act of genuine gratitude.[4] Like David, the man must have said in his heart: "What can I offer the Lord for all he has done for me?" His answer was with heartfelt praise and thanksgiving expressed with his words *and* by his actions.

Where Are the Other Nine?

When Jesus saw this man who had returned with sincere praise and thanksgiving, his heart was touched. Then his eyes scanned the

---

[4] Luke 17:15-16 AMP

faces of the crowd to see if there were other thankful hearts. Jesus looked in the direction of the village gates, but no one was running his way. Disappointment pierced the heart of Jesus as he asked,

> "Were not all ten cleansed (healed)? Where are the other nine? Was there no one (else) found to return and to give thanks *and* praise to God . . .? " (Luke 17:17 AMP)

Certainly, after the other nine were declared clean, they praised the Lord for their miracle of healing as they testified to family and friends. No doubt they expressed how thankful they were that Jesus had healed them. No doubt they were powerful witnesses whose testimonies glorified God. But there is also no doubt that they failed to express their praise and thanksgiving to the One who had healed them. They failed to put their thankfulness into action by returning to Jesus and falling on their knees before the One who had made them whole. Tune your ear once again to hear the disappointment in Jesus' voice: "Weren't ten men healed? Where are the other nine?"

How many times has Jesus answered our prayers? A job provided. A financial need met. A deliverance from an addiction. A loved one's salvation. A healed illness. We were thankful. We shared our testimony with others. We even offered a cursory thank-you prayer to God. But then did we just move on to our next request? Did our praise and thanksgiving echo the gratitude of this lone leper? He was intentional, deliberate, and profuse in his thankfulness, with enthusiastic words of praise and worshipful actions.

We need to convey that same depth of gratitude. We need to be just as intentional and earnest in offering thanks to God for all that he has done for us. Let us take care not to disappoint our Lord. To be thankful in both word and deed is such an important lesson we learn from this healed leper. This same lesson was also illustrated hundreds of years earlier by King David. Let's learn a little more about thankfulness from this remarkable man of God—a man whose heart's desire was to put his thankfulness into action.

Thankfulness in Action

In the latter years of King David's reign, he reflected again on how good God had been to him. Although he had penned over twenty psalms expressing his thankfulness, he wanted to put his gratitude into action. As he recounted his blessings, he noticed a great disparity. David resided in the splendor of a beautiful palace while the Ark of the Covenant, where God's presence dwelt, was housed in a tent. David decided to offer God a thank-you gift. He would build a glorious temple for the Lord. But there was a problem.

God was pleased with David's desire to build a temple, but David was a warrior king whose life was marked by bloodshed from battles too numerous to count. So, God gave the task of building the Temple in Jerusalem to someone else, to David's son Solomon. And this is what I love about David. Although it was David's desire to build that temple himself, when he learned that it wasn't what God wanted him to do, he didn't shut down or become offended. Instead, he expressed his thankfulness to God by supporting the one God had chosen to build this temple. From that point on, David committed himself to doing everything he could to ensure Solomon would be successful in completing this divine assignment. That's spiritual maturity. That's thankfulness in action.

For the next season of David's life, he focused his energy on acquiring the materials and manpower Solomon would need to build a magnificent temple to house the glory of the Lord. David started by seeking the face of God for the temple design, and it was given to him. David told Solomon, "Every part of the plan . . . has been given to me in writing from the hand of the Lord."[5]

With a set of temple plans complete, David next dedicated himself to procuring the carpenters, stonemasons and craftsmen, as well as to acquiring construction materials that would be needed. He then turned his attention to the operational needs by arranging the temple assignments for all the priests. Finally, David called together an assembly of the people and declared:

---

[5] 1 Chronicles 28:19NLT

"Using every resource at my command, I have gathered as much as I could for building the Temple of my God . . . And now, because of my devotion to the Temple of my God, I am giving all of my own private treasures of gold and silver to help in the construction. This is in addition to the building materials I have already collected for his holy temple. I am donating more than 112 tons of gold . . . and 262 tons of refined silver." (1 Chronicles. 29:2-3 NLT)

David had dedicated gold and silver from the national treasury, but now he desired to give generously from his personal account and encouraged the people to do the same. "Now then, who will follow my example?"[6] He challenged the leaders of Israel on behalf of the people to put *their* thankfulness to God into action. Inspired by their king, they gave over 185 tons of gold, 375 tons of silver, 675 tons of bronze, and 3,775 tons of iron.

David was pleased not only because of how much they gave but that they gave willingly. They didn't give out of obligation, but rather as an expression of their sincere gratitude for all that God had done for them. "The people rejoiced over the offerings, for they had given freely and wholeheartedly to the Lord . . ."[7] And their offering of thankfulness provided Solomon everything he needed to complete his divine assignment—to build God's glorious Temple in Jerusalem.

Lesson Nine

Voicing sincere words of gratitude to God is important. Being specific in thanking God for what he has done for us is necessary. Thanking him before we see the answer to our prayers demonstrates our confidence in him. Offering a sacrifice of praise touches the heart of God, but we must also put our thankfulness into action. This may mean giving our time and energy to meet the needs of others or using our gifts and talents to serve in the church. It may be expressed by

[6] 1 Chronicles 29:5 NLT
[7] 1 Chronicles 29:9 NLT

giving financial and prayer support to ministries that reach out to the sick, the poor, the hurting, or the unsaved.

Jesus no longer stands outside of that small Galilean village searching for the thankful hearts of nine healed lepers. But he still searches. From the Father's throne, he searches for those who cry from the very depth of their souls, "What can I offer the Lord for all he has done for me?" He searches for those who answer this question by lifting up their cup of salvation to *praise* the One who drank the "Cup of Sorrows" for us—-the One who died on the cross for mankind. He searches for those who offer a *sacrifice of thanksgiving* with heartfelt words of praise but also with actions of gratitude.

May his searching eyes light up as they fall on us, his faithful disciples who express thankfulness in word *and* in deed. Let us not disappoint the heart of our Lord as those nine lepers did so long ago.

Chapter Challenge

- Make a list of the things for which you are thankful, even the very simple things of life. Write them down or print a hard copy. As you begin to see the list grow, the reality of God's goodness in your life will come into focus.

- Now thank God for each one of these good things you have listed. Let the emphasis of your prayer today be one of thanking God instead of asking God.

- Be open to ways you can put your thankfulness into action by using the gifts, talents, and resources God has given you to bless those in need.

- Offer the Lord a genuine sacrifice of thanksgiving that pleases our Savior, that glorifies God.

Chapter 10

Embrace His Sword

They thought for sure this question would trip him up.

"Of all the commandments, which is the most important?"[1]

Surely he wouldn't be able to pick just one. And whichever one he did pick, they had already devised a comeback to discredit him. They couldn't stand Jesus. Each day, with every miracle he performed, with every sermon he preached, the number of people following Jesus and embracing his teaching increased. They could feel their grasp on the people slipping, their power position as religious leaders weakening.

To the Pharisees, Sadducees, and teachers of the law, Jesus was a dangerous agitator who needed to be stopped. Their strategy was to pose controversial questions about paying taxes, or divorce, or working on the Sabbath—questions designed to cause disillusionment among the people. No matter what question they posed, however, Jesus always had a profound answer to outwit them. Every trap they set backfired. But this time they were sure to ensnare Jesus with this question. With great anticipation, they wondered which commandment Jesus would select, so that the divisive debate could commence. Without hesitation Jesus replied,

---

[1] Mark 12:28

"Love the Lord your God with all your heart, soul, mind and strength. This is the first and greatest commandment. And the second is like it: Love your neighbor as yourself." (Matthew 22:37-39)

There was nothing to rebut. Impressed, one teacher of the law replied, "Well said . . . You are right . . ."[2]

Instead of singling out one superior commandment, Jesus summed up the essence of the Ten Commandments by stating how to love the Lord and how we are to love others. As difficult as it is, though, to love others as much as we love ourselves, the greater challenge is the first: to love the Lord with all our heart, soul, mind, and strength. We are challenged by the totality, the completeness of love we are to have for God. To love God with all our heart and soul is to love him with a passion and an all-consuming desire, to make him our priority, to seek his will. To love God with all our strength is to love him by our actions, by our works, and by the "fruit" he desires. But then there is loving God with all of our mind. That is the tricky part.

Had I been that teacher of the law, my follow-up question would have been: "How do I love the Lord with all my mind?" Because our mind is where doubt first plagues us, sidetracking our love for God and undermining our faith in him. It has been an issue from the very beginning in the Garden of Eden.

A Doubt Planted

Lucifer had fallen from the position of highest angel because he could not keep his prideful mind in check. He took his eyes off God and turned his gaze upon himself; his love for God was replaced with a fierce opposition. Lucifer's rebellion earned him the position of God's enemy. And he, along with a third of the angels, was cast from heaven, but his mission wasn't altered. His desire was to plant doubt

---

[2] Mark 12:32

into others' minds, inciting in them a rebellion against God. So when Adam and Eve arrived on the scene, they were his first victims.

Lucifer was not pleased with the position of authority God had given Adam and Eve, so he sought to destroy their close relationship. In the guise of a serpent, Lucifer engaged Eve in a conversation intending to sow doubts into Eve's mind. "Did God really say, 'You must not eat the fruit from any tree in the garden'?"[3] Eve corrected him. They could eat the fruit from any of the trees in the garden except the fruit of the Tree of Knowledge of Good and Evil. If they ate fruit from this tree, they would die. Lucifer responded with yet another seed of doubt:

> "You will not certainly die! . . . For God knows that when you eat from it your eyes will be opened, and you will be like God, knowing good and evil." (Genesis 3:4-5)

Lucifer—we know him better as Satan—planted the thought that God was keeping something good from Adam and Eve. And that if they disobeyed God and ate this special fruit they could be gods themselves.

> The woman was convinced. She saw that the tree was beautiful and its fruit looked delicious, and she wanted the wisdom it would give her. So she took some of the fruit and ate it. Then she gave some to her husband, who was with her, and he ate it, too. (Genesis 6:6 NLT)

Eve embraced Lucifer's deceptive reasoning with justifications of her own: the fruit looked appetizing, and it would give them wisdom. After all, isn't having wisdom a good thing? So she ate the fruit. Then without protest or hesitation, Adam took the fruit from Eve and ate it as well. How could Eve be deceived so easily, and how could Adam make such a blatantly disobedient choice? They failed to recognize the doubt Satan was seeding into their minds. Of the two voices they could choose from, Satan's or God's, whose was more trustworthy?

---

[3] Genesis 3:1-3

God's. Who did they know more intimately? God, of course. Yet they allowed doubt to creep in and undermine God's voice, God's truth. This led to rebellion, a sin that disrupted their relationship with God. And it all began in the mind.

The Power of the Word

Just like Adam and Eve, our minds can be filled with thoughts that cause us to doubt God, his promises, and his love. And it can lead to sin and disobedience. Perhaps this is why the apostle Paul exhorts us to "take captive every thought and make it obedient to Christ."[4] Taking a thought captive involves more than just capturing it. To "capture" means to seize, arrest, or apprehend, whereas to "take captive" goes beyond the capture: it involves submission. We are not just to capture those thoughts which oppose God, but also to bring them into submission and make them obedient to the Lord. But how?

Jesus gives us the answer by example. When he was tempted by Satan in the wilderness, at the end of his forty days of fasting and prayer, Jesus took captive every enticing thought Satan hurled at him. When Satan challenged him to satisfy his hunger by turning a stone into bread, Jesus took that thought captive with the Word of God, a scripture found in Deuteronomy 8:3:

> "No, the Scriptures say, 'People do not live by bread alone.'"
> (Luke 4:4 NLT)

Satan then attacked Jesus with the lure of power and glory. His response? The Word of God.

> "The Scriptures say, 'You must worship the Lord your God and serve only him.'"(Luke 4:8; Deut. 6:13)

---

[4] 2 Corinthians 10:5

Undeterred, Satan took Jesus to Jerusalem, to the top of the Temple and challenged Jesus to prove his identity.

> "If you are the Son of God," he said, "throw yourself down from here." (Luke 4:9-11)

Once again Jesus used scripture to rebuff Satan's temptation.

> "The Scriptures also say, 'You must not test the Lord your God.'" (Luke 4:13 NLT; Deut. 6:16)

By example, Jesus demonstrated how to use the Word of God as a sword to take captive every disobedient or rebellious thought. Jesus understood that his armor—his protection against the wiles of Satan, against any sinful thought—was the Word of God.

Armor of God

In the New Testament, there is a section referred to as the Epistles. These are letters written by early Christian leaders—like the apostles John, Peter, and James—letters to encourage and instruct believers. The most prolific writer among them, though, was the apostle Paul. One of the many letters he wrote was penned while he was under house arrest in Rome—a letter to the believers in Ephesus warning them that Satan seeks to sabotage every believer's faith. So Paul exhorts them, and us, to put on "spiritual armor" to thwart the schemes and strategies Satan wields against us.

Paul wrote this letter while he was under the watchful eye of a Roman guard day and night. Maybe that is why he used a soldier's armor in defining spiritual armor: The helmet of salvation. The breastplate of Jesus' righteousness. The belt of truth. The shield of faith. Peace that protects our feet, and the Word of God that is a sword.[5] Except for the sword, each piece of this spiritual armor is for protection and defense. But we can't make an enemy submit with a helmet or breastplate. We need an offensive weapon. The sword, the

---

[5] Ephesians 6:11

Word of God, is the very weapon Jesus used. He wielded the sword of the Word because he understood its power!

Our world was created when God used his words. God *said*, "Let there be light." And there was light. On each day of creation, God *spoke,* and everything he said came into being. And the Word of God, which brought forth the miracles of creation, is powerful enough to take captive any rebellious thought. It's powerful enough to thwart any thought of doubt or unbelief. Because it doesn't matter if you have just become a Christian or have been a Christian for decades; it doesn't matter where you are on the spectrum of spiritual maturity; all of us will experience thoughts of turmoil and anxiety that challenge our faith and love for God. No one is exempt—not even one of the great prophets of God, John the Baptist.

Are You Really the Messiah?

John the Baptist had a powerful ministry which prepared people for the arrival of Jesus as the Messiah. But near the end of John's ministry, he found himself languishing in Herod's prison. In despair, John sent two of his disciples to Jesus with a question. "Are you the Messiah we've been expecting, or should we keep looking for someone else?"[6]

What a strange question for John to ask. After all, he was the one who had declared that Jesus was *the* Messiah. He had baptized Jesus and heard God the Father's own voice declare Jesus to be his beloved Son. So why would John now doubt that Jesus was indeed the Messiah? Perhaps it was because Jesus performed miracles on the Sabbath day (something John would never have done). Or perhaps it was the report of Jesus eating with outcasts. Or maybe it was the realization that his life might end in a prison cell. The Bible isn't clear about why John doubted, but it is certain he was struggling with unbelief.

Jesus responded to John's doubts by sending John's disciples back with these words:

---

[6] Matthew 11:3 NLT

> "Go back and report to John what you hear and see. The blind receive sight, the lame walk, those with leprosy are cleansed, the deaf hear, the dead are raised and the good news is proclaimed to the poor." (Matthew 11:5)

He used these particular words to respond to John's doubt, because John was familiar with these prophetic words of the prophet Isaiah foretelling the acts of the true Messiah:

> Then will the eyes of the blind be opened and the ears of the deaf unstopped. Then will the lame leap like a deer and the mute tongue shout for joy. (Isaiah 35:5-6)

> The Spirit of the Sovereign Lord is on me *(the Messiah)*, because the Lord has anointed me to proclaim good news to the poor. (Isaiah 61:1-2)

Jesus sent the Word of God to John the Baptist as a sword to take captive those thoughts of doubt and unbelief, so that he could embrace with certainty once again the truth that Jesus was indeed the Messiah.

Our Sword

We, too, will be plagued with thoughts that cause us to question and doubt. Thoughts that keep us up at night. Thoughts that come racing in like a flood, robbing us of peace. Our faith becomes a struggle, our love for God wanes. It is in our mind, in our thought-world, where unbelief gains a foothold and doubt overwhelms us. It is in these moments that we need to use the sword of God's Word to take captive those thoughts and make them obedient to Christ and his will.

When unsettling questions abound and there are no easy solutions, use the sword of God's Word:

> If any of you lacks wisdom, you should ask God, who gives generously to all without finding fault, and it will be given to you. (James 1:5)

> "I (*the Lord*) will instruct you and teach you in the way you should go. I will counsel you with my loving eye on you."
> (Psalm 32:8)

When you are dealing with financial stress, consumed with fear and anxiety, God's Word declares:

> And my God will meet all your needs . . . (Philippians 4:19)

> . . . I have never seen the righteous forsaken or their children begging bread. (Psalm 37:25)

> Cast all your anxiety on him because he cares for you.
> (1 Peter 5:7)

When you are filled with thoughts of inadequacy and the fear of failure, use the sword of God's Word:

> I can do everything through Christ who gives me strength. (Philippians 4:13 NKJV)

> The Lord is my strength and my shield; my heart trusts in him, and he helps me. (Psalm 28:7)

When you are filled with despair and hopelessness, when everything is going wrong, use the sword of God's Word:

> . . . all things work together for good to those who love God, to those who are called according to His purpose.
> (Romans 8:28 NKJV)

When you have been treated unfairly—hurt to the core—and you are consumed with thoughts of how to get even, use the sword of God's Word:

> Do not take revenge . . . for it is written: 'It is mine to avenge, I will repay,' says the Lord. (Romans 12:19)

> And don't sin by letting anger control you. . . . For anger gives a foothold to the devil. (Ephesians 4:26 NLT)

> Pray for those who hurt you. (Luke 6:28 NLT)

When you struggle with tempting thoughts of sin, use the sword of God's Word to defeat them:

> But now you are free from the power of sin …
> (Romans 6:22 NLT)

> But you are not controlled by your sinful nature. You are controlled by the Spirit if you have the Spirit of God living in you. (Romans 8:9 NLT)

When you have asked forgiveness for your sins but are still consumed by thoughts of guilt and condemnation, take them captive with God's Word:

> If we confess our sins, he is faithful and just and will forgive us our sins and purify us from all unrighteousness. (1 John 1:9)

> Therefore, there is now no condemnation for those who are in Christ because through Christ Jesus the law of the spirit of life has set me free from the law of sin and death. (Romans 8:1)

And when you are plagued with thoughts of loneliness, remember God's Word:

> "Never will I leave you, never will I forsake you."
> (Hebrews 13:5)

> "Lo, I am with you always…" (Matthew 28:20 NKJV)

Lesson Ten

The Word of God is a sword. It can take captive any thought that would
— fill our hearts with doubt and unbelief.
— prevent us from being the person God has called us to be.
— stop us from doing what God has purposed for us to do.
— keep us from loving God with all our minds.
— hinder us from being devoted followers of Jesus.

But—and this is a big *but*—in order for us to use God's Word as a sword, we have to know God's Word.

We have to read it.
We have to prayerfully study it.
We have to meditate on it.

As disciples of Christ, we must plant the Word of God deep in our hearts so we are able to wield this powerful sword—a sword that helps us take captive any thoughts that would hinder our love for God and thwart his will from being accomplished in our lives.

Chapter Challenge

- Reflect for a moment: Are there thoughts that continue to bombard your faith, causing you to feel discouraged or make you unsure of your relationship with Jesus? Thoughts undermining your confidence in him? Thoughts of loneliness, unworthiness, or guilt? Thoughts of discouragement or confusion? What thoughts do you need to take captive?

- Search the Bible for verses of scripture that address your need. Use an online resource like *Bible Gateway, You Version,* or *Bible Hub* to help you locate scriptures. Read them, memorize them, apply them. (Note: Reading verses of scripture in various translations will help to broaden your understanding of them.)

- Personalize a scripture as a declarative prayer. For instance, if you are plagued with anxious thoughts regarding a difficulty your family is facing, apply the truth of scriptures like these to your situation: 1 Peter 5:7 ("Cast your anxiety on him because he cares for you.") and Psalm 32:8 ("I *(the Lord)* will instruct you and teach you in the way you should go.") You might pray:

"Lord, your Word declares that I can cast my cares upon you. And so right now I cast all of my anxiety about this situation upon you. I'm asking you to instruct me how to handle this family matter. Instead of looking at the problem and being plagued with fear and unrest, I place it into your capable hands, believing you will provide me with the wisdom I need and lead me in the right direction. You are in control. In the name of Jesus I pray, Amen."

- Wield the weighty weapon of God's Word to defeat any thought that would trip you up and cause you to stray from God's plan and purpose for your life.

Chapter 11

Embrace His Church

Four churches. In less than a one mile stretch of road near my home, on the same side of the street, there are four different churches: a large Apostolic church, a small Chinese church, a medium-sized Baptist church, and a little independent church. If you are looking for a church in America, whether you live in a city, suburb, or small town, it doesn't take long to locate one.

We have megachurches and quaint country churches. Seeker churches with lights and dazzling videos. Traditional churches with pews, choirs, and hymnals. Churches with steeples and stained-glass windows. Churches in strip malls and in schools. So, it's not unusual to conjure up an image of a building in a specific location when we hear the word *church*. We think of a *place* to worship God. But when Jesus used the word, he wasn't focused on a *somewhere,* he was focused on a *someone,* in fact, *"someones."*

We first encounter Jesus using the term *church* at a time when his ministry was gaining momentum. As his soul-stirring teachings electrified people's hearts, as his miracles of healing and deliverance amazed the multitudes, people questioned Jesus' true identity. Certainly, he was no ordinary rabbi or prophet. He was different. He had a unique presence and spiritual authority. There was all manner of conjecture: Could he be a great prophet like Moses? Or perhaps Elijah or Jeremiah? And Jesus was aware of their questioning. So he turned to his disciples and asked them, "Who do you say I am?" Peter's answer was immediate and emphatic: "You are the Messiah, the Son of the Living God."[1] Jesus then prophetically declared Peter's calling—what his ministry would be:

> "Now I say to you that you are Peter (which means 'rock'), and upon this rock I will build my *church*, and all the powers of hell will not conquer it." (Matthew 16:18 NLT)

And, indeed, these words came to pass. Peter along with the other disciples took leadership roles to establish Christ's church. But what I find curious is that Jesus would even use this word *church*. Remember, Jesus was Jewish: He was raised and immersed in the Jewish culture. You would think then that Jesus would have used the word *synagogue* or *temple*. These were terms his disciples would have been familiar with, too. But Jesus intentionally used *church*. The Greek word is *ecclesia*, and it means "called-out ones."

Jesus purposely used the word *church* because he was not interested in establishing great architectural buildings of worship. Rather, his focus was on people who would gather to worship the Lord—people who would be "called-out ones." His church would be those who have been called out from sin and into a relationship with Jesus. People who would be *in* this world but not *of* this world. In other words, people who would no longer seek to live their lives embracing the world's values but, rather, the values and morality exemplified by Christ.

This universal church consists of believers who worship the Lord no matter where they live, no matter where they gather. One local church may meet in a magnificent steepled cathedral, while another may meet in a simple outdoor tent. What is important is that we gather together as believers someplace. As believers we are part of his great universal church, but Jesus also wants his "called-out ones" to be part of a local church. We are not just to be believers who "*go to* church" but believers who "*are* the church"—believers who are

---

[1] Matthew 16:15-16

actively involved in fulfilling God's plan to share the message of salvation and live lives that glorify him.

The universal church is much like our natural extended family—family members to whom we are related by blood, marriage, or adoption, but whom we may rarely see or perhaps even know. But within this extended family is our immediate family—the family members we do know, those with whom we share our lives and experience life. And that is what the local church is to be: a church family where we are connected to fellow Christians as we become more connected to Christ, growing in love, and maturing in faith. So, let's delve a little deeper into the purpose of the local church family to see God's plan for us—we who are his called-out ones!

A Family Who Worships the Lord

When Jesus entered Jerusalem for the very last time, he rode on a young donkey as people laid palm leaves in his path, worshiping him with praises of adoration. As the sound of their praises rose in volume and fervor, the religious leaders became alarmed. Appalled that Jesus was accepting their adoration, they demanded he instruct the people to stop. But Jesus' response was not what they expected: "I tell you . . . if they keep quiet, the stones will cry out."[2]

That was a pretty bold and narcissist statement if Jesus were not the Son of God. But he is! And because Jesus was not just human but also divine, because he is part of the Trinity—God the Father, God the Son, God the Holy Spirit—worship was due him. And worship is still due him today. It is our privilege to offer unto Jesus words of praise, praising him for who he is and for what he has done. Yes, we can worship the Lord in private prayer, and we should. Yes, we can worship the Lord by living a life that pleases him, and we should. But we also need to gather together and worship him collectively.

How wonderful is God's promise that even when just two or three are gathered, he is there, and he will inhabit our praises.[3] It pleases

---

[2] Matthew 21:8; Luke 19:40
[3] Matthew 18:20; Psalm 22:3 KJV

the Lord when his "called-out ones" come together as a family to offer the worship of praise due him as sovereign Lord, as merciful Savior, as precious Redeemer.

A Family Who Values the Word of God

The Bible is a gift of God's words to us. In his letter to Timothy, his mentee, Paul reveals the specific purpose for the Scriptures—why the Bible should be read, studied, and applied:

> . . . they (the Scriptures) have given you the wisdom to receive the salvation that comes by trusting in Christ Jesus. All Scripture is inspired by God and is useful to teach us what is true and to make us realize what is wrong in our lives. It corrects us when we are wrong and teaches us to do what is right. God uses it to prepare and equip his people to do every good work. (2 Timothy 3:15-18 NLT)

First and foremost, the Bible reveals our need of a savior and that Jesus is our Savior—a savior we receive by putting our faith in him and what he accomplished for us on the cross. But then Paul goes further. Once we receive Christ, the Bible is to be a guidebook for how to live. Its teachings are to be the foundation of our faith, revealing what is true, what needs to be corrected in our lives, and what equips us for God's purpose and plan for our lives. The Bible must be valued in a local church family. It must be preached and taught. It must be studied and embraced. It must be applied. And to help us do this, God has specifically established pastors, teachers, and other spiritual leaders to make the Scriptures plain, to provide insight and guidance for everyone who is part of a local church.

> Now these are the gifts Christ gave to the church: the apostles, the prophets, the evangelists, and the pastors and teachers. Their responsibility is to equip God's people to do his work and build up the church, the body of Christ. (Ephesians 4:11-12 NLT)

After his resurrection, Jesus gave this prime directive to his disciples and to us—a directive that carries a great responsibility:

> "Therefore, go and make disciples of all the nations, baptizing them in the name of the Father and the Son and the Holy Spirit. Teach these new disciples to obey all the commands I have given you." (Matthew 28:29-20 NLT)

Not everyone is called to be a preacher who stands before a congregation delivering an inspiring message or a teacher who instructs a class sharing insights and encouragement from the Bible. But we are all called to preach and teach by what we say and how we live. All of us are to be disciples who in turn disciple others—nurturing and helping others become devoted followers of Christ. And, God has designed the local church to be that spiritual family where we can mature in faith, so that we are able to foster spiritual maturity in others.

A Family Who Prays

Jesus was a man of prayer—a man whose prayers weren't a recitation of religious words, but an intimate communication with the Father. Certainly, the Lord wants us to have those times of personal prayer, but he also wants us to be part of a church family where prayer is a valued priority—a local church that is a "house of prayer." Paul provides us with these words of instruction: "In every place of worship, I want men to pray with holy hands lifted up to God, free from anger and controversy."[4] Then in his letter to the church in Ephesus he writes,

> And pray in the Spirit on all occasions with all kinds of prayers and requests. With this in mind, be alert and always keep on praying for all the Lord's people. (Ephesians 6:18)

Paul's admonition to pray communicates the heart of God. He wants us, his children, to know his voice. One powerful way we can

---

[4] 2 Timothy 2:8 NLT

hear his voice is through prayer. And, it is in the local church where we can learn how to pray and have opportunities to pray with and for one another.

Recently my son-in-law was diagnosed with a serious brain tumor. When I received the news, my first response was to pray. My second was to contact members of my church family, asking them to lift him up in prayer. What strength and peace my family experienced knowing our church family was earnestly and fervently praying for him. They lifted a burden of prayer for us when we were in crisis mode. We were so grateful to be part of a church family who knows how to pray!

A Family Who Nurtures Your Calling

As the apostle Paul and his team traveled the first-century world preaching the gospel, they established many churches. But since church was a new concept, Paul used analogies to help these new Christians grasp how they were to function as a church. One powerful analogy he used was the body. To the believers in Rome, he wrote,

> For as in one body we have many members, and the members do not all have the same function, so we, though many, are one body in Christ, and individually members one of another." (Romans 12:4-5 ESV)

Every one of us is a part of the "body" of Christ, because we all have been joined to Jesus, who is the head of the body, the church. And just as our bodies are made up of many different parts—parts that don't look or work the same but are important to the whole body—the same is true in the church.

The analogy is powerful. We grasp the word picture and it is liberating: I don't have to be something God never created me to be! I don't have to try to be a foot if I am called to be an elbow. We understand this truth conceptually, but how does it play out in the reality of our lives? How do I know if I am a foot, a hand, even a toe?

And if I'm a toe, what does that mean in real life? I faced these questions in my early twenties.

I grew up going to church and was blessed to experience a genuine encounter with Jesus at a young age. I was saturated with God's Word by pastors who preached with power and teachers who taught with authority and insight. But as I began my professional career of teaching high school students, I felt compelled to seek God's plan for me as part of his church. "Lord, what part of the body am I? Where do you want me to serve? What ministry have you planned for my life?" I prayed for a clear and powerful answer, one with no question marks. "So, God, perhaps you could send a sign to reveal your plan for me? A voice from heaven? A prophetic word? Something, Lord!" But I heard nothing.

One Sunday morning my pastor announced that for the first time our church was going to hold a women's conference. Something quickened inside of me. I just knew that if I attended, God's plan would be revealed. So with great expectation, I attended this conference. The speakers were inspirational, the times of worship and prayer uplifting, but I didn't hear God's voice in any dramatic way. I was disappointed, and my countenance must have showed it, because one of the speakers, a woman I knew, asked why I looked so downcast. I explained I had felt God was going to reveal his plan and calling on my life through this conference, but I was leaving as I had arrived—without any idea.

She looked at me compassionately, and smiled, "Joy, do you want me to tell you what God is calling you to do?" My response was immediate and somewhat incredulous: "Of course, but do you really know?" She was emphatic: "Yes, I know. You are called to teach!" It was like bells and whistles went off inside of me. *Yes, of course!* By profession I was a teacher, and I knew I had a gift for communicating lessons in a clear and engaging way. But it wasn't until that moment that I realized that God—who created me, who knit me together—gifted me to teach not just for a career, but more importantly for his Church.

As I look back, I wonder why I was so blind to something so obvious. For some reason, I had the notion that whatever God would call me to do had to be something outside of my natural gifts—to prove that it was God, not just me, making something happen. I was corrected by a mature believer who cared about me because we had a relationship that existed in my local church. For you see, God uses Christians in the church to see gifts in us that we are too close to see. Certainly God can speak to you in some dramatic way about what part of the body of Christ you are called to be and how you can strengthen his Church. He may reveal his divine purpose for you through a word of prophecy spoken over you, through his still voice in a time of prayer, or through a mature believer who can see what you cannot see. The ways God can reveal his plan for your life are limitless. But whatever gifts he has given you—whatever calling he has designed for your life—it can be nurtured and developed in the local church.

After that conference, I approached the supervisor of the Bible classes in my church and volunteered to serve wherever I was needed. And where did my ministry as a teacher begin? With the toddlers! I poured myself into those children, and in time, other doors of teaching opened—first teaching young people and adults a Bible foundation class, then teaching at seminars, retreats and conferences.

God has a purpose for every believer's life. Every Christian has gifts to be used to strengthen and enlarge his Church, always with the mission of being disciples who disciple others!

Lesson 11

The local church is God's plan for us, his "called-out ones," to gather together where we can live our faith, grow in faith, and share our faith. Not alone. Not by ourselves. But as part of a spiritual family. The local church is a place to develop strong bonds with fellow Christians as we encourage and support one another in our pursuit to glorify the Lord. But I must add one word of caution. A perfect church does not exist. Just as there are no perfect natural families, there are no perfect spiritual families. We are individually in the process of being perfected, and the same is true of a local church.

Chapter Challenge

- If you are not attending a local church, I would encourage you to ask the Lord to guide you to a church where your faith will be strengthened and your relationship with him deepened. His guidance may come through an invitation by friends or family members to visit their church or, perhaps, as you view a church's website or listen to the pastor's podcasts. Be open to the many ways God can guide you to a church family.

- Get involved with a local church where you can put down spiritual roots and serve the Lord as you serve others with the natural and spiritual gifts he has given you. Find a church family who worships the Lord, values the presence of his Holy Spirit, embraces the Bible as the Word of God, believes in the power of prayer, and who compassionately bears one another's burdens.

- If you are already attending a local church, be more than an attender—get involved. If you are not sure where to start, contact someone on the pastoral staff and express your desire to discover and to use the gifts God has placed in you.

- Be a part of a church family who inspires you to be more than a believer in Jesus—to become a passionate follower of Christ who, in turn, can inspire others to do the same.

- Embrace his Church.

Chapter 12

Embrace Burdens

He was told that if he accepted this role he risked an abrupt end to his movie career. His response? "Each one of us has our own cross to carry. We either pick it up and carry it, or we get crushed under the weight of it."[1] In 2004, James Caviezel accepted the role to play Jesus Christ in the film, "The Passion of the Christ." As it turned out, his decision to accept the role was the easiest part. Caviezel explains,

> "This movie was torture right from the beginning in all forms. I was spit on, beaten, and I carried my cross for days, over and over the same road."

While filming the scourging, the lash of the whip accidentally tore a 14-inch gash on his back. During the crucifixion scene, while hanging precariously on a cross in nothing but a loincloth, he suffered hypothermia and a dislocated shoulder. He related that his feelings were anything but holy as he experienced the piercing pain of cold and fatigue. Yet as difficult as it was to experience this reenactment of Jesus' crucifixion, Caviezel said the film provides an incomplete picture of what Jesus actually endured. Had they gone any further into authenticity, the filmmaker feared it would have been too overwhelming for viewers. But when we read Jesus' prayer in the

---

[1] Interview with James Caviezel
https://www.beliefnet.com/entertainment/movies/ movie-was-torture-but-worth-it.

Garden of Gethsemane, it becomes apparent that the cross was almost too much for Jesus to bear.

Bearing the Cross

Alone, crushed with a burden of anguish and sorrow, with bloody drops of sweat forming on his brow, Jesus prayed not once but three times: "My Father, if it is possible, may this cup be taken from me."[2] Because Jesus is God the Son incarnate, we reverence his divinity. Yet, all too often we minimize his humanity. In this heartfelt prayer, with our eternal destiny hanging in the balance, Jesus the man asked God the Father for a reprieve from the cross. Can you take this cup of suffering from me? Can there be another way of salvation?

Going to the cross was not an easy choice for Jesus. His divinity had revealed his destiny, but it was his humanity that was crushed by what this destiny would require. Although each day of his ministry was filled with teaching in the synagogues, healing the sick, or mentoring his disciples, ever present was the burden of the cross. Long before this Gethsemane prayer, he told his disciples, "There is a terrible baptism ahead of me, and I am under a heavy burden until it is accomplished."[3]

When Jesus explained to his disciples in greater detail what this terrible baptism would require—how he would suffer greatly at the hands of the elders and religious leaders, be killed, and then raised from the dead—Peter reprimanded him, saying, "Heaven forbid! This will never happen to you!" Jesus quickly responded,

> "Get away from me, Satan! You are a dangerous trap to me. You are seeing things merely from a human point of view, and not from God's." (Matthew 16:23 NLT)

Why did Jesus react so harshly? Why would Peter's words be such a dangerous trap for him? Because they represented a choice Jesus

---

[2] Matthew 26:39
[3] Luke 12:50 NLT; Matthew 16:22 NLT

could make—a much easier choice—to avoid the cross and forego the suffering. Yet with focused determination, Jesus pressed on to Jerusalem, each day bringing him closer to the cross. And in those final hours of anguished prayer, he made the crucial choice to submit to the will of the Father: "Yet not as I will, but as you will."[4]

With these simple words, Jesus chose to embrace the burden of the cross without reservation. We witness his wholehearted commitment to the cross from the very moment the mob rushed through the garden gates. As Jesus rose from prayer, he heard angry voices: first faint, then louder, stronger. A contingent of Roman soldiers, temple guards, and Jewish officials burst into the garden with swords and clubs. He didn't flee, or struggle, or even attempt to hide his identity. Jesus openly identified himself, and Judas confirmed it with a kiss.

As the guards rushed in to arrest Jesus, Peter struck the servant of the high priest with a sword, cutting off his ear. Jesus quickly intervened and healed the man. Why perform this miracle, this act of compassion, while submitting to an unjust arrest? Because Jesus knew the cross was not about waging a physical war with swords of revolution. His destiny was not to lead a political revolt. His destiny was to embrace a cross that would bring spiritual victory—eternal salvation for mankind. That was the Father's will: to carry the burden of the cross.

Carrying the Burden of the Cross

Today we hold the cross in high esteem. It is displayed on the rooftops of our churches and in our sanctuaries. Men and women proudly wear crosses around their necks. But in the first century, the cross was a symbol of deep disgrace and dishonor. Crucifixion has been described as one of the most excruciating ways to die. It was invented by the Persians around 500 B.C., but perfected by the Romans. So ignoble and reprehensible, it was forbidden for a Roman

---

[4] Matthew 26:39 NLT

citizen to be crucified. Crucifixion was a display of extreme torture meant to intimidate anyone who would oppose or displease Roman authority. And, as in the case of Jesus, crucifixion often began with a scourging.

Stripped to his loincloth by a Roman guard, his back laid bare, Jesus was beaten with a flagrum—a short whip of leather strips, each with a metal ball or piece of bone attached. The lashes broke the skin on his back, from his shoulders to his buttock. With every consecutive lash, the pieces of bone or metal cut deeper, ripping his flesh, shredding it into a bloody mass of tissue.

After being beaten and mocked as the "King of the Jews," Jesus was required to carry his cross through the streets of Jerusalem to the place of crucifixion beyond the city gates, a place called Golgotha. The route the Roman guards took was not a short one. This was to be a public spectacle, a lesson for all the people of Jerusalem to witness. But as Jesus made his way through the streets, with each painful step, the weight of the cross became too much. The severe wounds of the scourging had sapped his strength. The rough-hewn wood of the cross grated against the open wounds of his back, and pain racked his body. He had lost too much blood. He was spent. He could go no further.

What a humbling experience for Jesus, the Son of God, to surrender to the frailties of a battered human body. He had authority to call the angels to administer the strength he needed. He held power to heal his broken body. But this was not part of the Father's plan. Not yet. So he chose human vulnerability as he collapsed under the weight of the cross. Jesus would need someone to bear the physical burden of the cross so that he could bear the spiritual burden of the cross.

Now the Roman guards were faced with a dilemma. Their prisoner couldn't carry his cross, and they weren't even close to the city gates. As members of the Praetorian Guard, they certainly weren't going to carry it for this despised Jew. The centurion in charge scanned the crowds lining the streets to watch the spectacle. Well aware of the week's Jewish holiday, the centurion knew that any

Jew who even touched this cross would be prohibited from the sacred Passover ceremonies, and he didn't want to spark a riot. Trouble with these Jews always seemed to be brewing.

Suddenly, a man caught his attention—Simon the Cyrene. Perhaps Simon's North African features or dress made him distinct. Whatever the reason, Simon was pulled from the sidelines and forced to carry a criminal's cross. Simon may not have even known who this Jesus was. After all, he wasn't from Jerusalem; he had most likely just arrived in town for the Passover. Yet, in total bewilderment, he found himself singled out to carry a cross for a man who claimed to be a king. In fact, his crime was written on a placard hanging around his neck. It read "King of the Jews."

At the centurion's command, Simon picked up the cross while Jesus struggled to his feet. Simon could see the agony each step inflicted on Jesus. He heard the taunts of the crowd. He heard women weeping and wailing, grieving at the suffering of this man. Finally, they arrived at Golgotha. Surely Simon watched as Jesus was nailed to the cross, not realizing the magnitude of what his death would accomplish.

The centurion's selection of this sideline spectator gave Simon the Cyrene an unexpected place of honor in the salvation story. For eternity he would be known as the man who carried the cross for Jesus. But it was an honor that could have belonged to his disciples.

A Missed Honor

Something is awry in the account of Jesus' journey of suffering through Jerusalem. Why did the centurion have to force a foreigner to carry this cross? Surely among the people lining the streets there were at least a few who had been healed or received a miracle from Jesus. Hundreds had sat on the mountainside and were captivated by his sermons, yet none were compelled to step in? But there are even more troubling questions: Where were the disciples? Where were Peter, James, John—any of them? Peter and John had followed Jesus to the high priest's palace where he was interrogated, but where were they when Jesus struggled through the streets of Jerusalem? Where were his disciples when the pain and loss of blood brought Jesus to the ground? And if they were there, why hadn't they immediately fought their way through the crowd to lift the burden for him?

Sadly, this was not the first time the disciples had missed an opportunity to help Jesus carry his burden. When Jesus went to the Garden of Gethsemane to pray, he had taken his disciples. He specifically asked James, John, and Peter to *watch* with him, to support him in prayer. Jesus told them he was crushed with sorrow and deep despair. He wanted their help to bear this burden in prayer. And what did they do? They fell asleep. Listen to the disappointment in Jesus' voice when he found them: "Couldn't you keep watch with me even one hour?" [5] Again he beseeched them to watch and pray.

Asleep in the Garden of Gethsemane.

Missing on the road to Golgotha.

Not one of his beloved disciples but, instead, a stranger was coerced to carry the cross for Jesus. In the months preceding his crucifixion, though, we see Jesus' response to four men who were not missing, but were very present, when—not a cross—but a friend needed to be carried.

Burdens Carried

The news of Jesus' arrival in Capernaum spread quickly. Which of the four friends first heard the rumor is not recorded, but once they learned the rumor was true, a decision was made. The rabbi named Jesus was in town. They had heard how his sermons stirred hearts, but also of his miraculous power to heal. He had cast out demons, made the lame walk, and caused the blind to see. He even had the power to raise the dead. And now he was in their hometown of Capernaum!

With hearts full of hope, they rushed to the home of a friend who was paralyzed. They would take him to Jesus to be healed. Each of the four men took a corner of his mat and carried the friend to the

---

[5] Matthew 26:38-45

house where Jesus was preaching. They came upon a large crowd blocking any entrance into the home. As they tried to wedge through, no one would give way. But they refused to give up. They noticed an outside stairway that led to the flat roof. Straining under the weight of the man and his pallet, they carefully navigated each step. Once on the roof, they removed a section of it and lowered their friend through the hole. Can you imagine the astonishment in that room as they watched a man on a pallet being lowered to Jesus? As the four friends leaned through that hole in the roof, Jesus looked up and acknowledged their faith.

> *Seeing their faith*, Jesus said to the paralyzed man, "My child, your sins are forgiven. . . . Stand up, pick up your mat and go home!" And the man jumped up, grabbed his mat, and walked out through the stunned onlookers."
> (Mark 2:5, 12 NLT)

These four friends showed their love by bearing the burden of their friend's paralysis. They didn't just bear a physical burden—though their solution was creative and not without perseverance—but also a spiritual burden. Jesus saw *their faith*.

Without those four friends, the man would never have arrived *at the house* where Jesus ministered. Without their perseverance, he would never have made it *into the house* where he was healed. And it was *their faith* to which Jesus responded! As four men carried the burden of their friend, it wasn't because they had been forced. There is no record that the paralyzed man had even requested their help. They took the initiative and embraced his burden out of love.

With Skin On

I once read a story about a little girl who was afraid to go to sleep at night. As soon as her mother left the room, the little girl would call out, afraid of the dark. Her mother turned on the night light and brought drinks of water, and innumerable trips were made to the bathroom. Stories were read, songs were sung, teddy bears and dolls were lined up across the bed, but nothing dispelled the little girl's fear. Running out of ideas, the mother finally said, "Darling, don't you know that God is here with you right now?" The little girl replied, "Yes, Mom, I know God is with me, but sometimes I need someone *with skin on*." This little girl had faith in God, in the intangible, but what she needed was a tangible expression of God—the loving presence of her mother. It wasn't the glass of water, or the stories, or the stuffed animals piled next to her that she really needed. What she needed was for her mother to lift the burden of fear. How? Just by being with her.

Lesson Twelve

God can lift any burden sovereignly, without any help from us. But over and over again we see God move to lighten the burdens of people by using us—we who have *skin on*. Paul wrote to the church in Galatia to "carry the burdens of one another, and in this way you will fulfill the law of Christ."[6] And what is the law of Christ? To love the Lord with all our heart, soul, mind, and strength but also *to love our neighbors as ourselves*. And one of the most powerful ways to love one another is to be that one *with skin on* and carry the burden of others. Whether it is someone in our family, church, community, or workplace, we must be sensitive to those around us with heavy burdens. We must be willing to step in and shoulder the cross that has become difficult for them to carry alone.

Bearing burdens may mean spending time with someone, just being a friend, taking someone out for coffee and listening. It may be cutting the lawn for a widow, making a meal, or helping someone financially. It may mean babysitting so a young couple can go out for a quiet dinner. At times bearing someone's burden may even take us out of our comfort zone—visiting someone in prison, comforting a family in tragedy, supporting someone diagnosed with a terminal disease. As disciples of Christ, it is our privilege to bear others' burdens. Unlike Simon the Cyrene, who was coerced by a Roman guard, we are to be compelled out of love.

---

[6] Galatians 6:2 NIV

But there is one more lesson here. There are times when we are the ones in need. Times when we need someone to help us, yet we shy away from sharing our burdens, believing that it shows a lack of faith or spiritual weakness. But remember, even Jesus needed help to carry his cross. Certainly, we must be disciples who do not stand on the sidelines but who *stand ready* to carry the burdens of others. But it also means we are willing to allow our friends—like the ones in Capernaum—to bear our burdens when we are suffering. Together, by carrying burdens for one another, we have the honor, like Simon, of being part of Christ's great salvation story.

Chapter Challenge

- Ask the Lord to make you more sensitive to the needs of those you come in contact with this week.

- Be willing to be the one *with skin on* to step in with an act of kindness, even when it requires sacrifice.

- And if the burden you carry becomes too heavy, reach out to those around you and accept their help without hesitation.

"Lord, help me to see the burdens others are carrying. So often the busyness of my life blinds me to the needs of others. Let me be willing to make the sacrifice of time, energy, and resources to help carry the burdens of those in need. And Lord, when I am faced with a heavy burden of my own, prompt me to let down my guard, lay down my pride, and accept help from others. Amen."

Chapter 13

Embrace the Fire

My husband and I drove twelve hours from Detroit to Boston to help our daughter and her family pack up for an eight-month sojourn in Rwanda. After packing and cleaning, and then more packing and cleaning, we drove twelve hours back to Michigan. It was work, but it wasn't a hardship. We wanted to help them, and it was help that wasn't demanded or even asked for; we offered.

Why sacrifice five days out of our lives when we had a long to-do list of our own? What was the motivation? It wasn't because we feared our daughter would be offended if we didn't help her. Rather, we did it out of love for her and for her husband and daughter. As counterintuitive as it may seem, and even though it required sacrifice on our part, there was a delight, even a joy from doing something that blessed her—that *pleased* her.

Which got me to thinking: Do I do things, what the Bible calls "good works," out of a fear of displeasing God? Or do I do them from a love that delights in pleasing him? Sometimes the good things we do—the good works that are to follow our faith—can be motivated by feelings of obligation and duty. The motivation shifts from a delight in pleasing the Lord to a fear of displeasing him. It's a slight but profound shift. The good works we do may not change, but certainly *the why* behind them must.

In the book of Revelation, we find seven letters written to seven ancient churches. These letters are full of encouragement, admonition, and correction, and they speak to us today as well. In the letter to the church in Ephesus, the Lord commends their hard work, their refusal to quit, their hatred of evil, their perseverance and courage—all attributes of devoted disciples of Christ. But there was one complaint.[1] They had walked away from their first love for the Lord. They had lost their passion. It wasn't that they didn't love him; the problem was that their love had waned.

All their doing, all their enduring, had sapped their enthusiasm for the Lord. There was no passion in the doing, and passion affects motivation—the *why*. God reminds us along with the Ephesians that he looks at the *why* as well as the *what*. To others, the doing may have been perceived as evidence of their passion, but God cuts through perceptions and sees the heart. With God, you just can't fake passion!

Keeping our passion for the Lord fresh and vibrant must be intentional. If we don't preserve our passion, if we don't stoke the fire of our love for him continually, we will become like the Ephesians. We will be commended for our works, but disappoint the Lord because they aren't done out of a heart of passionate love. And along the way, we may then discover that our fiery passion has been replaced with a numbing complacency, and complacency opens the door to sin. It can happen to the best of us, just as it did to Israel's greatest king, King David. In Chapter 8 we learned a lesson from David about how to respond with genuine repentance when we sin, but now let's look at how complacency set the stage for his sin.

King David

David was recognized as a "man after God's own heart," who expressed his thankfulness in both word and deed. Unquestionably, he was a man who fervently loved the Lord. Even as a mere teen, as Israel's army quaked in fear before the giant Goliath, David, with a passionate confidence in the Lord, felled this enemy with a sling and

---

[1] Revelation 2:1-6

a stone. When David was pursued by King Saul and his army, David turned to God for protection. Whether headquartered with his band of warriors in the desolate caves of Abdullam or in the provincial town of Ziglag, David was devoted to the Lord. Even his missteps during those fugitive years caused him to turn more fervently to God. When he was finally installed as Israel's king, David possessed an intense passion for the Lord.

Then David entered a season where his realm was secure. His enemies were retreating. And at this point in David's reign, he makes an uncharacteristic decision. Instead of leading his troops on the battlefield, he dispatched his commands from the safety of his cedar palace in Jerusalem. Everything was going well until . . .

> One late afternoon, David got up from *taking his nap* and was strolling on the roof of the palace. From his vantage point on the roof he saw a woman bathing. The woman was stunningly beautiful. (2 Samuel 11:2-5 MSG)

And David was stirred with desire for this woman. Consumed by lust, David committed adultery with Bathsheba. When she became pregnant, David embraced deception, which led to the murder of her husband. All in an attempt to cover his tracks and hide his sin. Yes, it was after a physical nap that David strolled on the rooftop, saw Bathsheba, and allowed lust to fill his heart. But before David ever took that afternoon nap, long before he took that leisurely stroll on the roof, David was napping *spiritually*. How did this happen? After all, this was the man who had passionately defied Goliath, shouting,

> "You come to me with sword, spear, and javelin, but I come to you in the name of the LORD of Heaven's Armies . . . Today the LORD will conquer you . . . This is the Lord's battle, and he will give you to us!"
> (1 Samuel 17:45-47 NLT)

As a warrior, he confidently declared God's faithfulness to protect him from King Saul's pursuing army:

"I look to you for protection. I will hide beneath the shadow of your wings until the danger passes by...He will send help from heaven to rescue me...My God will send forth his unfailing love and faithfulness."
(Psalm 57:1-3 NLT)

As a psalm writer, he penned,

One thing I ask from the Lord, this only do I seek: that I may dwell in the house of the LORD all the days of my life, to gaze on the beauty of the LORD and to seek him in his temple. (Psalm 27:4)

So, what happened to this passionate David? He napped. Complacency had replaced passion. Instead of seeking God for his next divine assignment, he was napping in the fulfillment of his current one. He was king, his realm secure, his armies strong. The Ark of the Covenant was returned to Jerusalem. His coffers were full. His fame was established. Then David napped, and his complacency allowed a mighty foothold for his lustful passions to usurp his spiritual fervor for the Lord.

When we examine the history of the kings who followed King David, we sadly see the same pattern. Asa, Josiah, and Jehoshaphat all began their reign with a wholehearted devotion to God. With great passion for the Lord, they tore down idols and reinstated God's commandments. But as the years passed, they took God's blessings for granted, and the routine of ruling led to complacency. Complacency led to compromise, and compromise bred unfaithfulness.

These great kings lost their passion for the Lord—they lost their first love—because they failed to intentionally guard their relationship with him. Their fervor for the Lord diminished as their need for him took a back seat. They took his blessings for granted and relied on their own wisdom, trusted in their own decisions, and gave in to their own desires. They became lukewarm toward God.

We, too, can fall into the same trap if we are not diligent. Our faith can morph into a religious routine that robs us of our passion.

The business and busyness of life can lead to spiritual complacency and a passionless love for God. We can still be active in our churches: teaching Bible classes, serving in the children's ministry, ushering on Sundays, working in the nurseries, visiting the sick, volunteering to serve meals to the homeless. We can still pray, read the Bible, tithe, and faithfully attend church services. But these things can become automatic and duty-bound, rather than the result of passionate love for the Lord. But God knew we would need help preserving our passion, so, God gave us a Helper—the Holy Spirit.

In Chapter 4 we learned how the Holy Spirit helps us become more Christ-like. In Parable of the Ten Maidens, Jesus illustrates how the Holy Spirit helps us keep the fire of passion for the Lord aflame.

The Parable of the Ten Maidens

During Jesus' time, a bridegroom would typically go to the bride's home for the wedding ceremony. The bride and groom, along with a company of guests, would then proceed to the groom's home for a great feast. Jesus begins the "Parable of the Ten Maidens" with the scene of ten young women waiting to join the wedding procession. They would have the honor of lighting the way to the wedding feast.

Their lamps were lit in preparation for the bridegroom's arrival. But the bridegroom didn't arrive when they expected, and they fell asleep. Suddenly, his arrival was announced and the procession began. The maidens awoke, but the oil in their lamps was running out and their lights were growing dim. To accompany the procession and light the way, they needed the fire in their lamps to burn brightly. Five of the maidens, whom Jesus called wise, quickly reached for the jar of extra oil they had brought. They refilled their lamps and joined the wedding procession. The other five maidens panicked. Their lamps were going out, and they had no extra oil. They needed to purchase more oil. Herein lies their problem!

While they were buying the extra oil, the wedding procession passed by. When they finally arrived at the bridegroom's door, the feast had already begun, and the bridegroom said they were too late to enter. They had missed their assignment and with it the opportunity to celebrate with the bridegroom. All because they had failed to prepare with extra oil—the oil needed to keep the fire in their lamps burning.

Jesus categorized these maidens into two groups: five wise and five foolish. But what distinguished the foolish from the wise? All ten wanted to be part of the wedding celebration. All ten had lamps. All ten had lamps that were lit. All ten were waiting. All ten even fell asleep. There was one thing, however, separating the wise from the foolish. The five wise maidens brought extra oil which they purchased in advance of the bridegroom's arrival. They were prepared for his unexpected delay.

The other five maidens were deemed foolish because they had only brought their lamps. Yes, their lamps were lit, but only with enough oil if the bridegroom arrived according to their timetable. They didn't think they needed extra oil. They thought that what they had in their lamps would be enough—that *enough* was sufficient. Then Jesus concluded the parable with this admonition: "Keep watch!"[2] Be prepared!

It's interesting that Jesus didn't admonish the maidens for falling asleep, but for lack of preparation. Five maidens were deemed wise because they knew their lamps could burn out and they prepared accordingly. They understood that enough is *never* sufficient. But the other five maidens were considered foolish because they were in town purchasing oil when they should have been in the presence of the bridegroom with the fire in their lamps burning brightly.

Extra Oil

God knows we will hit spiritual doldrums. There will be times, as we wait for the Lord's arrival with an answer to prayer or a revelation for that next step in our life, that we can grow weary. There are times

---

[2] Matthew 25:1-13 NLT

when the routines of life can cause us to slumber spiritually and our lamps become dim.

Then there will be times we face the unexpected. We never expect to hear a diagnosis of cancer or face financial difficulties or unemployment—yet it happens. We never expect to lose a child or a spouse, experience marital problems or divorce—yet it happens. We never expect to be hurt by a fellow Christian or betrayed by a church leader—yet it happens. The unexpected can chip away our faith. It can knock us off our feet and cause our lamps to dim. So Jesus' admonition is this: Never be without the *extra oil*. Before weariness sets in, before you encounter a delay or the unexpected, be prepared with the extra oil.

But what does Jesus mean when he instructs us to be prepared with that *extra oil*? Throughout the Scriptures, oil symbolizes the presence of the Holy Spirit. Having extra oil means that we aren't filled with *just enough* of the Holy Spirit, but rather with an *overflowing abundance* of his presence in our lives—guarding our hearts from complacency and compromise. This is how we keep from foolishly missing out on the best of what God has planned for us. The abundant anointing of the Holy Spirit kindles a fire of passionate love for the Lord, inspiring and empowering us to be obedient to this admonition of Jesus: "Be dressed and ready for service and *keep* your lamps burning."[3]

So how do we keep our lamp of faith burning brightly? How can we stay prepared with that extra jar of oil, the oil of the Holy Spirit? One powerful way is through praise, for praise keeps our focus on God and his will instead on us and our self-pleasing desires. Praise gives us strength to face "lamp-dimming" adversity and the challenges of life—a lesson learned from Paul and Silas who praised God even while imprisoned.

But why is praising God so powerful? Why does it bolster our faith in times of adversity? Why does it lead to being filled with an abundant, overflowing presence of the Holy Spirit—that extra jar of oil? Because when we praise God, his presence inhabits our praises.

---

[3] Luke 12:35

King David understood this truth when he declared, "But thou art holy, O thou that inhabits (*dwells in*) the praises of Israel." [4] There is powerful connection between praise and God's indwelling presence—a connection that is evident when we look back to the day when King Solomon, who had been given the divine assignment to build the Temple in Jerusalem, had finally completed the task. It was the day King Solomon and the Israelites were going to dedicate this Temple to the Lord.

The Temple in Jerusalem

During the fourth year of King Solomon's reign, he began constructing the Temple using the plan and resources provided by his father, King David. Solomon was guided by divine wisdom and motivated by his love for the Lord. After seven years, the structure was complete. And Solomon's singular desire was for this glorious Temple to be far more than a building admired for its architecture and grandeur. Above all else, he wanted God's presence to fill the Temple. So, on the day of dedication,

> . . . it came even to pass, when the trumpeters and singers were as one, to make one sound to be heard in *praising and thanking the Lord*; and when they lifted up their voice with the trumpets and cymbals and instruments of music, and *praised the Lord*, saying: For He is good; For His mercy endures forever,' *that then* the house, the house of the Lord was filled with a cloud, so that the priests could not continue ministering because of the cloud: for the glory of the Lord filled the house of God.
> (2 Chron. 5:13-14 NKJV)

As they praised God, his glory filled the Temple to overflowing. Not with just enough glory, but with an abundance of his presence. The glory of the Lord was so powerful, his presence so palpable, that the priests could not perform their duties, and the people were *ignited* with a passion for the Lord.

---

[4] Psalm 22:3 KJV

The praise of the people had invited and welcomed the presence of God to dwell in the Temple in Jerusalem. And now, thousands of years later, God still desires to fill his temple. But the temple God wants to fill with his abundant presence is different today. In 1 Corinthians we read, "Do you not know that *your body* is the temple of the Holy Spirit?"[5] Our bodies are now the temple of the Lord created to house the presence of his Holy Spirit. And when we praise him, this is his promise: to *inhabit* our praises. As we embrace the "fire" of the Holy Spirit through praise, his presence in us will ignite a passion for the Lord.

Lesson Thirteen

As disciples of Christ, it is our responsibility to guard our hearts from complacency. To be clear, complacency is not when we take an actual nap, a vacation, or just some time off to rest. After all, even God rested on the seventh day after six days of creating! We just don't want to nap spiritually. We must be intentional in keeping ourselves fueled and aflame by worshiping God with adoration and praise. Remember, when we embrace the in-dwelling, passion-producing "fire" of the Holy Spirit, his presence within us will ensure that we will be like those five wise maidens prepared with the extra oil that will keep our "lamps" burning—not dimly, but brightly.

Chapter Challenge

- Turn to these great psalms of David: Psalm 145 or Psalm 103. Personalize the praise found in these psalms. Whether you speak or write down these words of praise to the Lord, let them become your words, sincerely expressed from your heart.

- Listen or even sing along with worship songs that praise God for who he is and what he has done. Express these words penned by musicians as your words of adoration to God.

---

[5] 1 Corinthians 6:11

- With these words of praise, invite the Holy Spirit to be your Helper—to fill your "lamp" with the fresh and abundant oil of his presence—that the fire of your passion for the Lord will burn brightly!

Chapter 14

Embrace Prayer

They trembled in fear. Terror filled their hearts. God had entered the Garden of Eden. With fig leaves covering their nakedness, Adam and Eve were hiding from him. They had eaten fruit from the forbidden tree. God had warned them of the consequences, and they knew death was the penalty for their blatant disobedience. But now that God had arrived, would he finish them off, calling down holy fire to consume them? Would the earth open and swallow them up in a deep crevasse?

Incredibly, God doesn't strike them dead. Indeed, one day they would experience physical death, and God did declare specific judgments upon each of them. But God didn't wipe mankind off the face of the earth and start over. Nor did he abandon them in their sinful state. Certainly, if I had been God, I would have chosen one of these two options! Instead, at the same time that God declared his judgment for their sin, he also prophetically proclaimed a plan of salvation. There would be a child born whose heel would be bruised, but who in turn would crush the head of the serpent.[1]

When Adam and Eve heard these words, they didn't understand. Adam and Eve had no idea that this promise would be fulfilled when God would send his Son to be that child, born of a woman, who would crush the power that Satan held over mankind because of sin.

---

[1] Genesis 3:15

They didn't understand the depth of suffering and sacrifice he would endure. But they did understand it was a promise of salvation: through this child, God would make a way for mankind's redemption. They understood that the God who had given them life was truly a God of immeasurable love. To make a way of salvation even though man flagrantly disobeyed God—that is divine love. But the picture of God's love is incomplete until we consider one more act he performed at this moment of judgment: "And the Lord God made clothing from animal skins for Adam and his wife."[2]

God didn't instruct Adam to make this sacrifice. No, God sacrificed the animals. Then he covered Adam and Eve's physical nakedness with clothing made from the animals' skin and covered their spiritual nakedness with the animals' blood. This small act of care and concern, documented in one simple sentence, gives us an insightful glimpse into the immensity and depth of God's love—the same love his Son, Jesus, demonstrated when he walked this earth.

The Love of Jesus

Over and over again, Jesus expressed his great love for humanity as he ministered to people day after day and hour after hour, with miracles of healing and deliverance. Whether it was a demon-possessed child, a lame man, a leper, or a woman with an incurable disease, Jesus ministered with love and compassion. Yet one of the more poignant expressions of his divine love occurred when Jesus spent his last night with his disciples. He did something they never expected.

> He (Jesus) had loved his disciples during his ministry on earth, and now *he loved them to the very end....So* he got up from the table, took off his robe, wrapped a towel around his waist, and poured water into a basin. Then he began to wash the disciples' feet. (John 13:1, 4-5 NLT)

---

[2] Genesis 3:21

Jesus expressed his profound love for his disciples by washing their feet. To us, this seems to be a strange act of love. And indeed, when Jesus began to wash the disciples' feet, they too, thought it was strange, even bewildering. Not because having feet washed was so unusual; it was a customary experience in the Jewish tradition of the first century as an act of service and hospitality. What stunned the disciples was who was doing the washing. Nothing would have been out of the ordinary if any one of the disciples had washed Jesus' feet. In a tradition-shattering move, Jesus, their respected master and teacher, was down on his knees washing their feet like the lowliest household servant. Jesus humbled himself out of love for his disciples, so that they would learn a powerful lesson—the necessity to serve out of love.

Jesus washed their feet not because their feet were physically dirty. He washed his disciples' feet because of his concern for their spiritual walk. His time with these twelve men was coming to an end. He knew the time for them to fulfill their divine purpose as apostles, establishing the church here on earth, was about to begin. Jesus knew, however, that to fulfill their calling, they needed the same heart of love for people that he had. They would need a love that would motivate and empower them to serve not just those who were lovable and likeable or rich and powerful. They were called to minister to the lost, the needy, the suffering, and the outcast. After washing their feet, Jesus then gave them this command—a command they were to embrace as his disciples, a command that was to become the hallmark of their ministry:

> Remember the ways that I have loved you, and demon-strate your love for others in those same ways. Everyone will know you as My followers if you demonstrate your love to others. (John 13:34-35 The Voice)

The way Jesus loved them was the standard of how they were to love others. That bar was raised as they witnessed the Messiah get down on his knees and wash their feet. All twelve of them, including the one who would betray him to the Jewish leaders. Eleven disciples would remember how Jesus washed the feet of his betrayer with the same love and care with which he had washed their feet. Even though Jesus knew betrayal was already firmly in Judas' heart, he still washed Judas' feet. Even though Jesus knew he would be betrayed by Judas' kiss of false love, Jesus still washed his feet. Even though he knew Judas loved money more than the Lord, Jesus still washed his feet. He washed Judas' feet because the core of Christ's character is love.

Jesus loved all of them, deeply and fully. He loved them despite their bickering, lack of faith, shortcomings, denials, and even betrayals. The Lord's love is not a cautious love; it is a lavish love. It is a self-sacrificing, servant love, demonstrated by his life and culminating in his death. And the command given to these first-century disciples remains true for us today:

> Watch what God does, and then you do it, like children who learn proper behavior from their parents. Mostly what God does is love you. *Keep company with him and learn a life of love. Observe how Christ loved us.* His love was not cautious but *extravagant.* He didn't love in order to get something from us but to give everything of himself to us. Love like that. (Ephesians 5:1-2 MSG)

We are to love like Jesus: we are to love others with an extravagant love. And the Scriptures declare we can learn to love like Jesus by keeping company with him. But how do we do that? *By spending time with him in prayer!* We know this truth, but we struggle to embrace it. Constantly, we juggle the demands of life with the need to set aside time for prayer—time to keep company with Jesus. It is a struggle, though, that is not unique to us. In the first century, we see this same struggle played out in the life of a woman named Martha.

Martha and her sister Mary weren't part of Jesus' inner group of twelve disciples, but there is no dispute that they were disciples of Christ, devoted followers who were dear to Jesus. Along with their brother, Lazarus, they were considered his close friends. Whenever

Jesus was in Bethany, he stayed with them. And on this occasion, many guests had gathered in their home to hear Jesus teach.

The Essential Thing

Pots and pans are clanging in the kitchen. Water is boiling on the stove. Bread is baking in the oven. The table needs to be set and the salad made. And where is Mary? Martha loved hosting fine dinners, but with so many guests—and among them such a special guest and friend, Jesus—she was frazzled. She needed help.

Leaving the kitchen for a moment, Martha spied Mary, sitting at Jesus' feet. Martha was frantic with all the details of preparing this meal to honor Jesus, and Mary was just sitting there. With a stomp in her step and a huff in her voice, Martha marched into the gathering room and implored Jesus,

> "Lord, doesn't it seem unfair to you that my sister just *sits* here while I do all the work? Tell her to come and help me." (Luke 10:40 NLT)

But Jesus' response was not what Martha expected. Jesus didn't rebuke Mary and instruct her to assist Martha in the kitchen. Instead, he chided Martha that she was consumed with putting on a dinner, when dinner was not the important thing. Then Jesus continued, "One thing only is essential, and Mary has chosen it."[3]

Mary's choice was to sit at Jesus' feet and be transformed. Martha was so distracted by the details of serving a great meal that she failed to value the presence of Jesus. She had the opportunity to keep company with Jesus, but instead chose to be busy in the kitchen. She chose to let her gift of serving take precedence over his presence. Mary had the same choice, but she chose the better thing. She chose what was essential—to be with Jesus. Mary followed the example set by Jesus himself, who always made the choice to keep company with God the Father.

---

[3] Luke 10:42 MSG

Embrace His Call

Sometimes we get so wrapped up in awe at the miracles of Jesus and the wisdom of his teaching that we fail to grasp how essential it was for him to keep company with his heavenly Father. If you read the Gospels closely, you realize how often Jesus carved out time for private prayer. After hours of ministering, Jesus would slip away from the crowds, even from his disciples, so he could pray. He would get up early in the morning or stay up through the wee hours of the night to pray. For him, prayer was not reserved for a moment of crisis in the Garden of Gethsemane; it was his custom to pray.

> Then, accompanied by the disciples, Jesus left the upstairs
> room and went *as usual* to the Mount of Olives (to pray)…
> (Luke 22:39 NIV)

The Lord's Prayer was given to us because the disciples saw the importance of prayer to Jesus. They saw the power of his praying, not just in the miracles he performed or in the wisdom of his teachings, but also in the love relationship he had with God the Father. Jesus loved to pray—to keep company with the One who is love. Surely, this must have been the kind of relationship Adam and Even once enjoyed with God in the Garden of Eden but, sadly, lost. Thankfully, this intimate relationship can be enjoyed once again. Because of Christ's sacrifice, we can withdraw from those around us and find that place of private prayer and keep company with the Lord. We can "sit at his feet" and enjoy a spiritual intimacy with the One whose presence can fill us with extravagant love. A love that is

> . . . patient and kind. Love (that) is not jealous or boastful
> or proud or rude. It does not demand its own way. It is not
> irritable, and it keeps no record of being wronged. It does
> not rejoice about injustice but rejoices whenever the truth
> wins out. Love never gives up, never loses faith, is always
> hopeful, and endures through every circumstance.
> (1 Corinthians 13:4-7 NLT)

We can learn to love like this. We can learn to love like Jesus by making prayer essential in our lives. Not just when we face a crisis or need to make a major decision, but more importantly to enjoy his presence—a presence that fills us with his love.

Lesson Fourteen

After the fall of Adam and Eve, what they missed most, I imagine, was that barrier-free access to the presence of God they had once enjoyed. How they must have longed to keep company with him in the cool of the evening as they once had. But because God is love, his desire was to restore that relationship. So he sent Jesus to make it possible for us to keep company with him, to spend time in his presence, to be touched by his love—a love we need to be able to genuinely love others as Jesus did.

We can be the most gifted preacher, the most insightful teacher, the most knowledgeable prophet, the most successful evangelist, the most generous giver, but if we don't have his extravagant love for others, our acts of service are but noise to God.[4] We become like Martha, serving not with love, but with complaint in our hearts.

Jesus desires that we love one another fully and deeply, because as his disciples, we are to be known by our love—his love reflected in us and through us. We must choose, therefore, the essential thing—to keep company with him in frequent and intimates times of prayer. So start today!

Chapter Challenge

- Make a plan. Decide when and where you can pray. Put it on your calendar or in your phone with an alert. Perhaps start with just five, ten, or fifteen minutes a day. Use online sources like access devotionals to get started. You can also use the Lord's Prayer as a pattern by focusing in on five key words: praise, purpose, provision, pardon, protection.[5]

---

[4] 1 Corinthians 13:1-3

[5] Rea, Tony, "When You Pray," podcast, www.cccsterling.org, January 2018

- First look at how Jesus opened the prayer: *Our Father, who art in heaven, hallowed be thy name.*

These are words of **praise,** extolling the holiness of God's name. Once again we see the importance of praise in our relationship with the Lord. So start your prayer by praising our holy God for who he is: for his greatness, his power, his love, his mercy, his grace. Remember how the power of praise invites a fresh indwelling of God's presence into your life.

- Jesus continued: Thy *kingdom come, thy will be done on earth as it is in heaven.*

Pray for God's will, his **purpose,** to be accomplished in your life, in the lives of those you love, or in the situation you are facing. Pray for God's will to be done in the lives of those he places on your heart.

- Then Jesus said: *Give us this day our daily bread.*

Here, Jesus gives us permission to ask for his **provision** in our lives. So ask him to supply your needs as well as the needs of others. Ask for the provision of healing—physical, spiritual, emotional, and relational. Ask for wisdom and guidance. The apostle Paul writes, "Do not worry about anything. Instead, pray about everything."[6]

Also remember to ask *with* thanksgiving. Along with your requests, thank God for what he has done for you and for what you believe he can do!

- Now, the challenging part of the Lord's Prayer: *Forgive us our debts as we forgive others.*

---

[6] Philippians 4:6 NLT

During your time of prayer, ask God to bring to your remembrance any sin. Confess it and genuinely ask for forgiveness, and he will **pardon** you.

But with his forgiveness comes his mandate that you, too, must make the *choice* to forgive those who have wronged you—to pardon them. And often it is a choice we won't *feel* like making, but it's a choice that he blesses, as we do for others what he has done for us.

- Next Jesus said: *Lead us not into temptation, but deliver us from evil.* Now he instructs us to pray for the Lord's **protection.**

  Ask him to protect you from the enemy of our soul who uses temptation to trip you up and plant seeds of doubt to discourage your faith.

- He then concludes the prayer: *For thine is the kingdom and the power and the glory forever. Amen.*

  Words of praise once again!

- Praise, purpose, provision, pardon, protection, and then praise once again! A powerful pattern for prayer, a powerful way to keep company with Jesus—the One who has chosen us, the One who fills us with his love.

Embrace His Call

The Pharisees followed Jesus. They followed him into the synagogues to debate his divinity. They followed him into the streets of
Jerusalem to contest his Sabbath miracles. They followed, but for the
most part, these Jewish leaders—the religious elite of Israel—were not
true followers of Jesus. Not that there weren't any who believed,
especially after the resurrection of Lazarus. Indeed, there were
religious leaders who could no longer deny that Jesus was the
Messiah. They, however, remained silent because of the threat of
being expelled from the synagogue and losing their position of power
in this Jewish community. They were believers, but they rejected his
call to be a disciple—a devoted follower of Christ.

> Yet at the same time, many even among the leaders
> believed in him. But because of the Pharisees they would
> not openly acknowledge their faith for fear they would be
> put out of the synagogue; for they loved human praise
> more than praise from God. (John 12:42-43)

Yet despite the Pharisees' opposition to Jesus, the number of
people who chose to be his followers increased daily. In fact, the
number of disciples following Jesus surpassed those of John the
Baptist. Jesus' ministry had gained unprecedented momentum.
Thousands were enthralled as they listened to his teachings and

witnessed his power to heal and deliver the sick and oppressed. All was well until one day Jesus taught about bread. He proclaimed, "Anyone who eats the bread from heaven will never die."[1]

At first, this teaching about bread was appealing. These Jewish disciples were well-versed in the history of the wilderness Israelites. They remembered how God had miraculously provided bread from heaven called manna. It was physical bread the Israelites ate daily that provided nourishment as they traveled through the wilderness. But Jesus was talking about a new kind of heavenly bread that would bring eternal life. If they ate this heavenly bread, they would live forever. Now he had their full attention. Their interest in this bread was intense, until Jesus revealed that *he* was that heavenly bread:

> "I am the living bread that came down from heaven. Anyone who eats this bread will live forever; and this bread, which I will offer so the world may live, is my flesh..." (John 6:51-52 NLT)

> "I tell you the truth, unless you eat the flesh of the Son of Man and drink his blood, you cannot have eternal life within you." (John 6:53-54 NLT)

> "Whoever eats my flesh and drinks my blood remains in me, and I in him." (John 6:57 NLT)

We read these Scriptures already knowing how Jesus established the emblems of the bread and cup in Communion, the Lord's Supper, as the means by which we embrace this truth—to "eat his flesh" and "drink his blood." But these first-century disciples only knew the Mosaic Law, and to eat human flesh and drink blood was absolutely forbidden. These words of Jesus were offensive and flew in the face of everything they had been taught. And many people rejected him because of this teaching. "From this time *many* of his disciples turned back and no longer followed him."[2]

Not just a few, but many walked away from their call to be his disciples. They walked away from the Lord because of a difficult

[1] John 6:47 NLT
[2] John 6:66 NLT

teaching. As those disciples turned away, Jesus then turned to the Twelve and inquired if they were going to abandon following him as well. Would they, too, turn their backs on Jesus? Peter quickly responded,

> "Lord, to whom would we go? You have the words that give eternal life. We believe, and we know you are the Holy One of God." (John 6:67-68 NLT)

Peter and the other disciples didn't understand this truth any better than those who walked away. It was just as offensive to them, but they clung to an overriding certainty: They knew Jesus was the holy One of God, the Messiah. They knew that somehow, some way, there was divine truth in his words. This teaching would not deter them from following Jesus.

If Peter and his fellow disciples had turned away because of this difficult, seemingly offensive teaching, they would never have enjoyed the Last Supper with Jesus when he revealed its meaning. They would never have become the apostles who established Christ's church here on earth. They would have missed fulfilling their divine purpose, fulfilling Christ's Great Commission—to disciple the nations.

Keep Running the Race

The apostle Paul instructs us to run with endurance the race that is set before us.[3] Each of us has a specific race to run—a divine purpose with divine assignments for our lives. But no one's assignment is identical to anyone else's. No one's race is exactly the same, but every race does require endurance. There will be times for all of us when being a disciple of Christ will not be easy. The race, the following, will become difficult. There will be obstacles in our path and offenses that can stop us in our tracks. Like those first-century Christ followers, there may be times when a spiritual truth in God's

---

[3] Hebrews 12:1 NLT

Word will be difficult to grasp, even puzzling. And the enemy of our soul will seek to use what we don't fully understand to plant doubts that tempt us to quit, to stop *following*.

Don't give in to that temptation. No matter the offense, no matter the difficulties, no matter what truth you don't fully grasp, follow instead the example of Peter and the other ten disciples—just keep following Jesus. Trust him and press on. Finish the race he has marked for you! Don't allow anything to keep you from *embracing his call* to be more than a believer—to be his disciple, a devoted follower of Jesus Christ.

Group Discussion Questions

Chapter 1: Embrace His Love

1. What experiences or interactions in life can make us feel insignificant to God?

2. As believers who have made the choice to follow Jesus, why is it important to know that we are loved by God?

3. What are some ways that God has demonstrated his love for you?

A scripture that reminds me I am loved by God: _____

_____

Chapter 2: Embrace Your Identity

1. Why is it important to grasp the truth that you are a child of God?

2. What blessings are ours as his adopted children?

Embrace His Call

3. What "bread" do you have need of today? Comfort? Peace? Guidance? Provision? Share your need with the group or just with one person in your group. Take a moment and pray for one another.

A scripture that reassures me that I am a child of God: _____

_____

Chapter 3: Embrace His Presence

1. We read in James 4:8 (NKJV), "Draw near to God and He will draw near to you." What does it look like to "draw near to God?

2. It was fear that caused the Israelites to withdraw from God's presence. What keeps us from making the choice to draw near to God?

3. Why must we be intentional about developing a lifestyle of drawing near to God?

A scripture that encourages me to embrace God's presence: _____

_____

Chapter 4: Embrace His Expectation

1. Why does God's expectation for us to become Christ-like seem impossible to achieve?

2. How does the Holy Spirit help us become more like Christ?

3. Why is it important for a disciple of Christ to bear *both* in- and out-of- season "fruit"?

A scripture that motivates me to bear much fruit: _____

_____

Chapter 5: Embrace His Plan

1. Why do you think that God doesn't reveal all of the details of his plan for our lives right from the beginning?

2. Look back to the moment that you first accepted Christ as your Savior. Now reflect on where you are now in your relationship with him. What aspects of his plan has he revealed to you? What doors has he opened? What people has he used to guide in your faith journey?

3. Why is it difficult for us to patiently wait in the present as God prepares us for our future?

4. What is the most meaningful lesson that you learned from the way Joseph responded to God's plan for his life?

A scripture that inspires me to trust God's plan for my life: _____

_____

Chapter 6: Embrace Adversity

1. When you face adversity in your life, what tends to be your initial response?

2. Why does God allow adversity in our lives even when we are doing exactly what he has instructed us to do? Why would it be an expression of his love?

3. Why is it important for us to praise God even when we are experiencing adversity in our lives? What can we praise God for when the adversity causes heartbreak and pain?

A scripture to lean on when I am experiencing adversity: _____

_____

Chapter 7: Embrace His Chastening

1. What is the difference between "perfecting" chastening and "corrective" chastening? How do we know the difference?

2. Have you ever experienced corrective chastening? If so, in what ways was it beneficial to you?

A scripture that states that God's chastening is an expression of his love for me:

_____

_____

Chapter 8: Embrace Repentance

1. What are the signs of an unrepentant heart?

2. What is the difference between regret, remorse, and repentance? Why is it important that we know the difference?

3. As a Christ-follower, why is regret and remorse for our sins not sufficient? Why is repentance necessary?

A scripture that explains the power of repentance: _____

_____

Chapter 9: Embrace Thankfulness

1. Why do we tend to do more asking than thanking God when we pray?

2. How can we become more intentional with our thankfulness?

3. Besides being thankful when we pray, how can we express our thankfulness? Why are just words of thankfulness insufficient?

A scripture that reminds me to express my thankfulness to God:

_____

Chapter 10: Embrace His Sword

1. Read 2 Timothy 3:15-16. List the reasons that the Bible has been given to us?

2. How do we know that the Bible is God's words to us, not just fabricated by the scheme of men?

3. Have you ever used a verse of scripture from the Bible as a "sword" to take captive a thought of unbelief, fear, or doubt? If so explain.

4. If you were to encounter someone who has not read the Bible but expresses the desire to begin, where would you suggest he/she should start? What translation of the Bible do you enjoy reading?

A scripture that describes the power of the Scriptures as a sword:

_____

Chapter 11: Embrace His Church

1. Why is it significant to understand the root meaning of the word "church?"

2. Why do you think some believers refrain from being part of a local church? Why is that a dangerous choice?

3. Why does a disciple of Christ need to be a participant, not just a spectator/attender in a local church?

4. If you are part of a local church, what benefits have you experienced?

A scripture that confirms the necessity of being part of a local church:

_____

Chapter 12: Embrace Burdens

1. Why do we hesitate at times to share the burdens of others?

2. Why do we at times refrain from sharing our burdens with others?

3. Share an experience where you have borne someone's burden. What sacrifice was required? How were you blessed?

4. Share an experience where someone bore a burden for you? How were you blessed?

A scripture that tells why we are to bare each other's burdens:

_____

Chapter 13: Embrace the Fire

1. How does praising God stoke our passion for the Lord? What can you praise God for today?

2. When do we tend to nap spiritually?

3. Have you ever experienced a time when you napped spiritually? What caused you to "nap?" How did you get back on track?

4. Why is embracing the presence of the Holy Spirit in your lives vital to your spiritual growth as a disciple of Christ?

A scripture that documents an experience by believers in whom the "fire" of the Holy Spirit fostered a passion for the Lord:

_____

Chapter 14: Embrace Prayer

1. How is prayer and genuinely loving others (even the unlovable) linked together?

2. Why do we often struggle with being devoted to prayer? What struggles have you experienced?

3. How can you "grow" your prayer life? How can prayer become part of your lifestyle?

A scripture that inspires me to pray: _____

_____

Embrace His Call

1. What do you do when you are faced with a difficult truth or scripture from the Bible?

2. What should we do when a Christian leader we look up to is tripped up by sin? How do we keep following Jesus when we are crushed by their failure?

3. What blessings do you receive when you make the choice to embrace Jesus' call to be his disciple—to follow him?

A scripture that encourages me to continue to follow Jesus even when the following becomes difficult.

_____

Discussion Tools for Group Leaders

Throughout the year, my husband and I attend what our church refers to as a Life Group. We meet with a small group of couples on a regular basis to study God's Word through a book study or a short video series. We read, discuss, and pray together. The texts we have studied have helped us deepen our understanding of the Bible and fostered a passion to continue to follow Jesus.

Because book studies in a small group setting have been a blessing to us, I have included Group Discussion Questions to be used with *Embrace His Call.* It is my hope that whether your group consists of new believers, mature believers or those somewhere in between that the questions will spark rich discussion causing the truth of God's Word to create a deeper devotion to our Lord Jesus Christ. As an educator, though, I know that sometimes just posing a question to a group leads to a deadly silence or to the same person answering all the questions! To promote inclusive discussion, I want to share two effective facilitation tools you can use with your group. The first is "Think, Pair, Share" and the second is "Consensus Circle."

Facilitation Tools

"Think, Pair, Share"

- The group leader poses one of the discussion questions and instructs the participants to *think* of an answer on their own.

Embrace His Call

- After providing adequate time for participants "think" of an answer, the group leader instructs each person to "pair up" with someone in the group and *share* their answer s with each other.

- The group leader then has each partner group *share* their answers with the whole group.

"Consensus Circle"

- The group leader provides each participant with an index card and places them in groups of three or four.

- The group leader selects one of the discussion questions and instructs each person to write three or four possible answers to that question on the index card.

- Once this task is completed, the group leader instructs each person to pass their index card to the person on their left (or right) in their group. Then they are to select one of the answers that is most meaningful to them, which they star or make a check mark to indicate their choice.

- Once completed, the index card is passed to the next person. The process continues until all the cards have been read and marked.

- The group leader then asks those who received three or four stars (checks) by one of their answers to share their statements with the whole group. Time should be allowed for people to respond to the statements that are shared.

ACKNOWLEDGEMENTS

Over the course of my life, there have been disciples of Christ who have influenced me in profound ways—none more so than my parents, John and Bernice Hughes. They weren't pastors or teachers, evangelists or missionaries. No, they were humble servants of the Lord in our local church. They demonstrated daily with love, compassion, and generosity what it means to be more than believers, to be devoted followers of Jesus. Although I can no longer thank them in person, I want to acknowledge publicly their legacy of faith that continues to inspire their children, grand-children, and great-grandchildren—a legacy that made this book possible. Thank you, Mom and Dad!

I also want to extend a genuine thank-you to my good friends, Al and Linda Lawrence and Wendy Jones, and to Christine Hughes, my sister-in-law, who read the first drafts of this book. Their input encouraged me to stay the course and finish what I had started.

And then there is Emily Gehman, my adept editor, who challenged me to be a better writer by sharing my story. Thank you for your insight and critiques that forced me to dig deeper and to keep the thread of this book woven from beginning to end.

Lynda Stallwood, Megan Rea, and Pastor Terese Rea, you were instrumental in helping put the final touches to the manuscript. I especially appreciate your feedback concerning the Group Discussion Questions. Your experience with Bible studies provided the guidance I needed. Thank you.

Linda Cadariu, Your expertise is a gift I treasure. Thank you for proofreading the manuscript, but above all for your friendship. I know one day I will read the book you are destined to write.

To my daughter Patricia, thank you for your creative input. I am grateful for your guidance with the artwork, but most of all for your timely words of encouragement.

A special thank-you to my daughter Jennifer, whose computer expertise kept me from lofting my laptop across the room! Your willingness to help touched your mother's heart.

I am also grateful to my daughter Allison, a devoted follower of Jesus. The way you embraced adversity this past year has inspired us all.

And to my husband, Joe, you were the one who first challenged me to step out of my comfort zone of teaching into this world of writing. Thank you for the gentle push I needed to complete what God had placed in my heart to do.

CPSIA information can be obtained
at www.ICGtesting.com
Printed in the USA
LVHW090048021219
639094LV00002B/602/P